Curator /Creative Director : Sijuan
Art Director : Jacky Low
Project Editor : Vivian Toh
Editor : Susuasli
Project Designer : Vvhy Yip

Produced by :
Bigbros Workshop
For more enquiries, kindly email to us :
info@bigbrosworkshop.com

Publish by :

GINGKO PRESS

Published in North America & Europe by:
Gingko Press, Inc.
5768 Paradise Drive, Suite J
Corte Madera, CA 94925, USA
Phone (415) 924 9615
Fax (415) 924 9608
email: books@gingkopress.com
www.gingkopress.com

ISBN: 978-1-58423-311-4

To quote Karim Rashid, design is no longer a word or a profession, it is a philosophy, a doctrine, a way of living, a modus operandi, a way of being that will one day be seamless with existence.

In fact, mankind has striven throughout history in the name of creation. The desire for innovation, expression and beauty has been timeless. Take the mystical pyramids in ancient Egypt, still standing majestically before the eyes of the world. The past is constantly reminding us of idealized models for life, continually adding to our conceptions for the future. A shift after World War II led to the postmodernism era, which ultimately led to the 1980s when we started experiencing graphic design.

Take Undoboy. Although an ardent follower of the superflat postmodern art movement, an interest group influenced by manga and anime, and founded by Japanese artist Takashi Murakami, Undoboy went a step beyond, creating interactive 3D toys, his Super-Bastard Box Art Characters, winning himself and his agency a string of accolades in the process.

With the introduction of user-friendly design software to the masses, more and more of us are acquainting ourselves intimately with the way that things around us can look. As our knowledge and choices open up, we see the growing need for practical and beautiful things, like the chandeliers of Marcel Wanders, chairs by Tunto Design and portable Joyn designs by Hinoshi Tsunoda of Design Code.

Much thought has been given to improving living standards by injecting art into our lives, be it on DVDs (courtesy of 5 Inch), iPod skins (45 iPod Cases), USB flash drives (mimoco) or even our used cardboard boxes (box doodle projects) and public spaces (see Ryan Frank's Hackney Shelf installation/public art/furniture project).

Beauty, you would think, is abstract. Yet, sometimes, it takes the eyes of a designer to turn what seems to be of no value into something valuable, to extend the shelf life of an old, used product, to give it another story to tell. At the same time, sustainability is no longer a responsibility of just the manufacturer but that of all parties, from creator to end user. The idea of material acquisitions is slowly being juxtaposed with the appreciation of space.

All these current movement and more, you will get a bird's eye view with over more than 57 international artists and over 100 original design ideas showcased here in Stuffz – Design In Material. It has itself stemmed from our own curiosity for functional, well-designed products and our eagerness to unearth the best stuffz around.

So without further delay, indulge yourself in the upcoming pages. We believe the more you read, the more you'll start seeing design lingering in your dreams, sticking fast to your aspirations and benefiting from your contributions.

CONTENTS

location / Vancouver • British Columbia • Canada

website / www.contexture.ca / www.45ipodcases.com

DIGITAL MEETS ANALOG:
45IPODCASES

www.45ipodcases.com

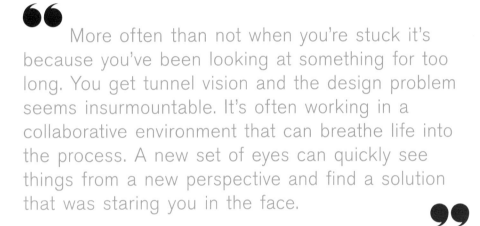

" More often than not when you're stuck it's because you've been looking at something for too long. You get tunnel vision and the design problem seems insurmountable. It's often working in a collaborative environment that can breathe life into the process. A new set of eyes can quickly see things from a new perspective and find a solution that was staring you in the face. "

– 45 iPod Cases (Contexture Design) –

Consumers are starting to ask what it took to get an object into their hands and if anyone was exploited in the process. These questions are readily answered when it comes to products designed by Canadian-based Contexture Design, which are often hand-made from locally sourced materials. The folks here believe that hand-made and well-designed items translate into real market value.

Based in Vancouver, Contexture Design is the brainchild of Trevor Coghill and Nathan Lee. The two started out studying landscape architecture at University of British Columbia. In between semesters, they hunted for jobs in the belief that the only way to get started was to get a desk job at a large design firm and rendering someone else's idea. At a point however, they decided, no matter how tough the decision was, to skip this first step and work up the ladder all by themselves.

Perhaps through their studies of the relationship between human civilization and the environment, Contexture puts a lot of store on doing what's sustainable rather than what's popular and has worked a lot with reclaimed materials. Be it landscape, graphic or industrial design, the materials they work with are often laden with histories and sentiments, which thus often impart exceptionally strong character to the results.

A case in point is Trevor and Nathan's 45 iPod cases which, using origami, the Japanese art of paper folding, transforms old vinyl discs into recyclable iPod cases. Durable, distinctive and named after the record-playing speed of course, 45 iPod cases are made up of reclaimed 7-inch vinyls, as well as a clear plexiglass window, cork liner and felt padding (40% recycled fibres).

New iPod cases use reclaimed vinyl albums to protect digital music players

created by / Contexture Design
The cases are known as '45', after the typical playing speed
of 7-inch vinyl records.

Made to fit iPods ranging from 20 GB to 80 GB, the cases are
composed of thermoformed vinyl records, felt padding of 40 per
cent recycled fibers, cork and a plexiglass window.

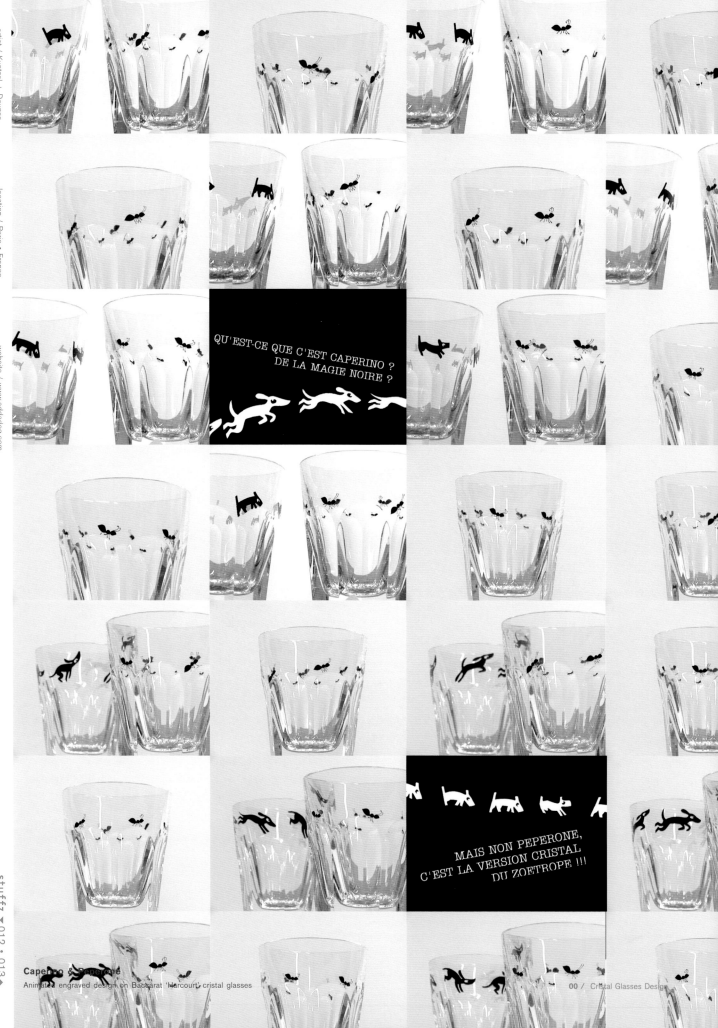

QU'EST-CE QUE C'EST CAPERINO ?
DE LA MAGIE NOIRE ?

MAIS NON PEPERONE,
C'EST LA VERSION CRISTAL
DU ZOETROPE !!!

Caperino & Peperone
Animated engraved design on Baccarat 'Harcourt' cristal glasses

CACHE OF VIRTUE:
ADD A DOG
www.addadog.com

> "For us, virtuosity is highly desirable (in our work). It's nothing to do with complexity or challenge but rather, the power to make something out of nothing appear superior and exceptional.
>
> – Add A Dog –

In the early years of computer imaging, their name was a byword for virtuosity in this field. Paris-based Add A Dog production and post-production company is the centre of operations for Olivier Kuntzel and Florence Deygas. The latter has a background in classical animation for movies and fashion illustration, while the former indulges in all things design and communication.

Add A Dog houses two visual artists and a pair of faithful shiba-ken dogs, a photo shooting studio and a post-production atelier. When asked why dogs are significantly etched on their company name and all across the website, they say, "Dogs have personalities. In France, a pet is like a member of the family. They have a name, people take care of and respect them. We consider our characters as virtual pets too."

According to them, design is a wide word that incorporates the categories of "stylists" and "creators." Kuntzel and Devgas include themselves as part of the latter. Like stylists, they create a trend. Unlike

stylists, they make mistakes.

This following statement explains their ignorance on the ongoing design scene: "We have no fixed vision about it, but we can say that we deeply miss 'virtuosity'." No doubt virtuosity is a strong word to be used in design but we couldn't agree more with these people.

Their characters Caperino & Peperone in the opening title sequence of the Steven Spielberg movie, Catch Me If You Can, were built upon a storyline and life. Among other creations of theirs are the Winney mystification program, the Veuve Clicquot advertising campaign, the Nokia 8800 TV commercial and the Parliament artist pack project which they made in the years the studio was making its name.

It was probably the meeting with Mr. Yakushiji from the Tohokushinsh Film Corporation during their first trip to Japan 13 years ago that particularly enlightened them however. The wise man said that beauty will glow from the contrast of simplicity created by Add A Dog's style

and high level projects. Many years after, Add a Dog created a flow of synergy with Sarah from Paris' Colette shop, which promoted Caperino & Peperone to the world.

Besides that, Kuntzel and Devgas, who state Matisse and late Stefano Lonati as inspirations, enjoy the ad-hoc experiences in designing remarkable characters for TV animations and movies.

"What we are trying to do is to create stories that organically develop from real life. We don't know when, how the story will end," the duo explains, adding that we humans have filled our lives with imaginary friends. Precisely.

"That's why our characters have come in pairs: Caperino & Peperone, Winney & Loosey and even Com-Pet because you need a minimum of two Com-Pets to communicate," Kuntzel adds. Furthermore, 2 is a good number. It invites dialogues and encourages reflection.

Caperino & Peperone

Artist Collection with Birkenstock Papillio, Summer 2007

Caperino & Peperone

14 animated designs embroided on Lacoste Polos
coordination by / Colette

Embroideries on Lacoste observe sneakers
coordination by / Colette

01
02

01 / Slippers Design
02 / Lacoste Series Design

Caperino & Peperone

Collette 10th Anniversary window display
with Caperino & Peperone exclusive products

Isetan x Vogue Nppon Presents

'Caperino & Peperone,
A Round World' Exhibition

00 / 'A Round World' Exhibition

Isetan x Vogue Nppon Presents
'Caperino & Peperone, A Round World' Exhibition
Inside Display at 'The Stage'

Caperino & Peperone

Special Version of the RAR Eames Rocking Chair
coordination by / Isetan

Caperino & Peperone
'Back To Bones' Sunglasses with LindaFarrowVintage
coordination by / Colette

Caperino & Peperone
Hat 'Caperino & Peperone'
created by / Stephen Jones
coordination by / Colette

Caperino & Peperone
400% Medicom Be@rbrick
coordination by / Isetan

Caperino & Peperone
Design applied on Repetto Shoes
'BB' model • left and 'Zizi' model • right
Exclusive Edition, coordination by / Colette

Lampes Mi-Cha

design by / Olivier Kuntzel

00 / Lamp Design

ROSE
OSER
EROS

Veuve Clicquot Rose Champagne
drawing by / Florence Deygas

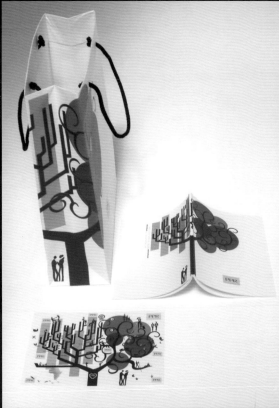

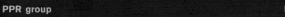

PPR group

'The Tree with a Double Structure'
Concept & design from the ID movie by
Kuntzel + Deygas, applied on goodies

Parliment Cigarettes

Limited Edition Artist Pack 2004

01 / Packaging Design
02 / Goodies Design
03 / Cigarettes Packaging Design

00 / Duvet Design

> "We take clippings from the plant. Some of our bestsellers are really some of the ugliest plants in real life. It's how you interpret them that makes them beautiful."
>
> – Amenity –

Little was known about Amenity when it was started by Nicole Chiala and Kristina de Corpo in 2005. Even then however, being green and sustainable were the important criteria in design. It doesn't hurt then that Nicole and Kristina are nature lovers to the core. Together they created the Amenity Home line, as well as a more recent line of bedding called Amenity Nursery complete with organic fibre blankets, pillows and prints, through which little children will come to love and appreciate the joys of nature.

Starting out anew and feeling fearless, Amenity focused on botanically inspired designs, with images digitally taken from the woods and their garden then applied onto bedding material as prints. Nicole and Kristina had no idea how hard it was to print artwork that was 5 x 7 feet wide onto beautiful percale cottons. Fortunately, a printer liked their idea and was keen to help. Since then, Amenity has amassed several different prints on purely organic, 320 thread count cotton.

This venture into the textile industry occured as they were stepping out from the wilderness of their upbringing in the wood-lands of rural Minnesota (Kristina) and Northern California (Nicole). Kristina was very close to her modernist, Norwegian grandmother who introduced her to the world of Scandinavian designs featuring woodland landscapes, dramatic seasons and evocative light. Nicole, meanwhile, had tasted adventure with nature while growing up on a farm with her family. They were friends in an art school who'd parted ways in search of their dreams, but ended up in Los Angeles where they saw a way to combine their passions.

The prints they make are a sole reflection of themselves and where they come from. The woods are the place their thoughts are clear and realigned. Even when they are not working, they collect inspirations from the native botanical gardens of California or a nursery to just slow down and appreciate the gift of nature.

That's Amenity's goal: to give people a relaxing feeling of bringing nature and its solace home. Every designed home accessory and bedding is intricately made of organic fibre and well developed to resemble nature and its subtlety.

01 / Leaf Duvet Design
02 / Twig Duvet • Close up
03 / Drift Duvet • Close up

00 / Pillows Design

location / Los Angeles   website / www.artecnica.com

Garland Light

DESIGN TO INSPIRE:
ARTECNICA
www.artecnicainc.com

> " The Design with Conscience campaign promotes, directs and sponsors collaborative exchanges between leading designers and artisan communities to create meaningful design that challenges people to adopt a deeper, more sensitive way of thinking about objects. "

– Artecnica Inc –

With a special interest in environmental issues, Artecnica has been pooling internationally recognised designers from all over the world for a series of collaborative stints for their ongoing programme called Design with Conscience. This deep sense of awareness towards the environment keeps LA-based Artecnica busy, often utilising recycled products and fusing these objects with design for better value.

As of print, Design with Conscience is ready to launch "Re-Imagining the Workshop", an exhibition celebrating five years of collaborative exchanges with the likes of Tord Boontje, Stephen Burks, Estudio Campana, Hella Jongerius and Emma Woffenden. In general, the campaign has been efficient in educating the public about the environment through art and technology that can be found in its range of designer products.

Committed to enchant, inspire and transform, the company continues to explore the world of uncertainties, where our environment is globally at stake. Where the public is concerned, the vital part in making Design with Conscience a dream achievable lies in the production of the products.

Artecnica has made a profound shift towards more sustainable and environmentally friendly material in the belief that "easy-ship flat packed products can reduce transport", thus minimising environmental impact and stimulating depressed economies.

Other than Design with Conscience, Artecnica also handles projects involving influential artists and designers. Take for example, their line of art collectibles created by Takashi Murakami, a veteran designer from Japan. As described by Artecnica, Murakami skilfully melds high and low art along with mass production in creating an international art toy marketplace for the younger generation.

From one project to another, Artecnica's transformation is strongly felt and discussed by international media such as New York Times, Time, Wallpaper, Harper's Bazaar, House & Garden, Architecture Digest and The Columbus Dispatch to name a few.

Garland Light

Come Rain Come Shine

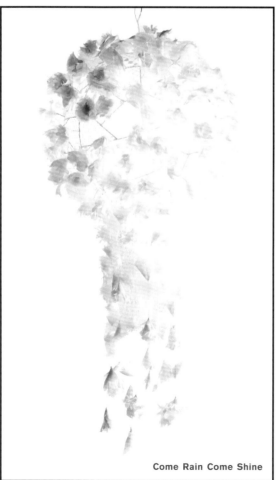

Come Rain Come Shine

Come Rain Come Shine

artist / Jackie Fan

location / Los Angeles

website / www.artecnicainc.com

Ivy Panels

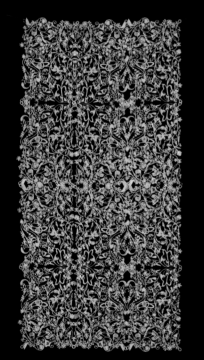

Untill Dawn Curtain

Untill Dawn Curtain

Untill Dawn Curtain

Book Of Light

HANDMADE IN ITALY:
BABBU
www.babbu.it

Cristina Onofri never studied fashion nor does she like reading fashion magazines. Yet, she managed to impress many others with her self-designed Babbu, not least when it debuted as a collection of women's apparel and accessories at Paris' WHO'S NEXT Exhibition in 2005.

Her love-hate feelings for fashion have always contributed to Cristina's idiosyncratic creations.

"Maybe it's funny but I don't even buy magazines because I always see the same style," she says. "I guess that you can flip through an old magazine of five years thinking that it's a new one."

The fashion designer asserts that she doesn't try to differentiate herself in the industry because the only important thing for her to do is "to follow my style and create stuff that people would deem as fashionable and like them as much as I do."

Hence, Babbu was born as a sweet white teddy bear with an honourable duty of going all the way to the rest of Europe and Asia to introduce people to its lovely world of cute, feminine clothes and colourful accessories.

Each collection has its own theme, which is primarily inspired by dolls with childlike motifs in bright colours sewn onto wool, cashmere shoppers and other equally su-perior fabrics. These are also used to make brooches, necklaces, tiny bags and glass jewels, which make up Babbu's love-ly accessories collection.

Till now, Cristina has produced six collections. Also, several of her characters have been featured in the "Made in Italy" fashion design book and her successes highlighted in Rome's TV RAI's "Look At You" programme.

00 / Accessories Design

00 / Wallpaper Design

SECOND GENERATION:

BANGKOK2

www.bangkok2.com

"To add more fun to my work, I try to experiment with mathematics to generate various (graphic) elements. The results can be quite striking sometimes.

– Ekalak Vorranartpankul, motion artist of Bangkok2 –

In the dawn of digital art and technology in Thailand, Bangkok2 generates a new breed of design and visual communication works. Bangkok2's ever-growing list of clients is testament to its commitment to effective yet experimental design, as compiled in their online design book.

Foreseeing that the local design scene had yet to reach its full potential, Nattavut Luenthaisong and Thanawat Chongmahakul had in 2000 founded Bangkok2, which also meant "second generation", to cultivate talents.

There are many impressive works from Bangkok2 such as Tsunami/2 Days in Thailand, a memorial in photographs of the Tsunami aftermath taken by Sasis Suwonpakprak. Formerly just specialising in 2D graphics, Bangkok2 now thrives in interactive design too. Check out Girl6, an interactive short film presented in association with Plog7 which publicly acknowledged

the multitude of sins usually shunned by society. In 2006, Bangkok2 also provided the graphic identity for the 5th Annual Thailand New Media Art Festival (MAF'06) and presented a workshop at Chulalongkorn University on the merging of art, technology and commercial interests.

Design is now widely accepted as part of the everyday aesthetic by Thai people, says Ekalak Vorranartpankul who started out young and soon emerged as the motion artist for Bangkok2. Today, Ekalak is working on a new project for Bangkok2, which puts his graphic and illustration works onto Inkjet stickers.

Bangkok comes across as an economic hub where culture is fully embraced by close to nine million city dwellers. Here, Bangkok 2 works hard to bring to its people a new kind of aestheticism with a unique fusion of Thai and western cultures.

artist / Ekalak Vorranartpankul

location / Bangkok • Thailand

website / www.bangkok2.com

BIGGIES ON EXPERIMENTAL GRAPHICS:

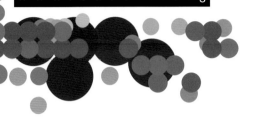

BASE-V

www.base-v.org

> " We have a weird thing for handmade projects; sometimes it's on a huge wall, sometimes it's just printing non-stop a series of silk-screened drawings, or sometimes it's digital. Anything that you can put your hands on. Hand-made. "
>
> – Base-V –

Brazil's city of Sao Paolo is home to many talented individuals, not least experimental graphics group BASE-V, made up of Danilo Oliveira, David Magila, Anderson Freitas, Rafael Coutinho and its latest addition, Javier Costamajor.

The members of BASE-V like to work on different levels of productions to make any work they produce original and versatile. The team usually runs through a series of experiments on various themes, styles and mediums to come out with a clear definition and direction. On a more profound level, they always look for relevance in everything they do. The possibilities are endless.

These big boys love working together and being able to act on the same piece from conceptualisation to execution. Of course there have been disagreements and misunderstandings stemmed from different views and backgrounds but that's okay because occasions like these keep them together.

Since its conception in 2002, BASE-V has been working up the ladder in the design industry and getting stronger. For example, they have had several published editions of "V" Magazine and "Maguila" digital magazine under their belts, in addition to special appearances in StereoPublication, 45//30 Magazine, Blank Magazine and Simples Magazine. They have also participated in exhibitions in London, Colombia and Brazil. BASE-V's clientele includes FIAT, Trama Records, Next Five Minutes, Tactical Media Brazil and Projeto Nave.

website / www.base-v.org

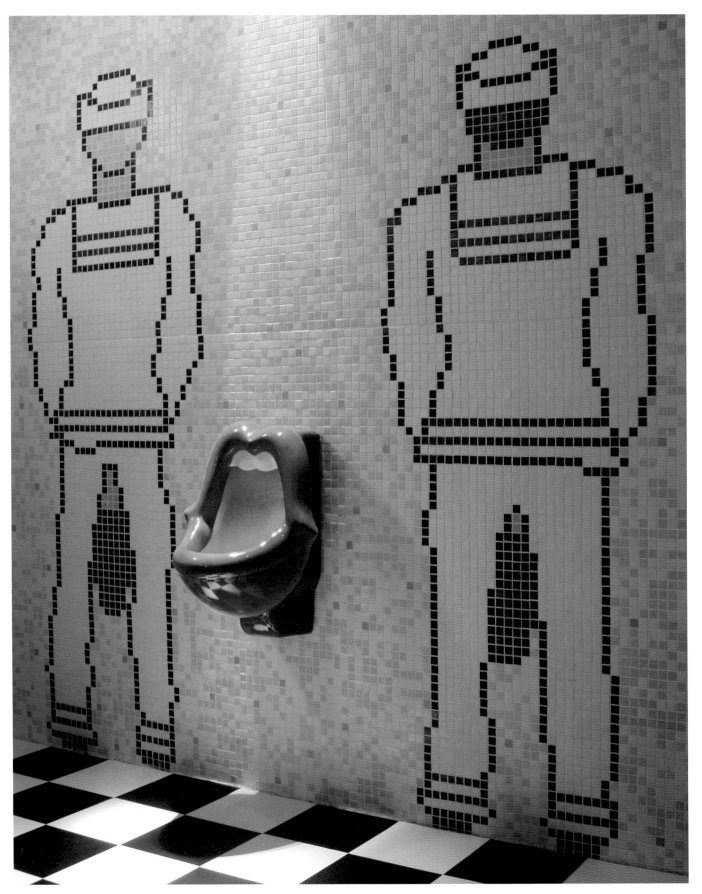

photography by / Daan Verschuur

00 / Toilet Products Design

SENSUAL VISUAL:
BATHROOM MANIA!
www.bathroom-mania.com

“ The project ('Kisses' urinal) involved bringing more color and fun into the bathroom to enrich the experience of the daily ritual of bathing. ”

– Bathroom Mania! –

What are those pouty red lips doing in the men's toilet with mouth wide open, you wonder. Sure enough, visiting the bathroom is no longer a dull experience with the great things created by Bathroom-Mania! The cheekiness of its 'Kisses' urinal is just one part of Bathroom-Mania!'s entire range of products, creatively imagined for that little boys' room and little girls' room in all our lives.

It was in September 1999 that Meike van Schijndel decided to combine her studies in illustration at Hogeschool voor de Kunsten (Utrecht, the Netherlands), with her father's knowledge in architecture to create something unusual for her final project.

Upon her discovery of the bathroom's potential to become a lucrative business, she was imagining illustrative designs on the surfaces of toilet bowls, washbasins, bath tubs and tiles. In her reckoning, the bathroom was starting to evolve from a purely functional space into a crucial element of living. Brian Golsteijn meanwhile possessed a degree in Industrial Engineering and Management Sciences with a wide background in business consultancy.

Together, Meike and Brian have, since 2001, headed this new and innovative design firm with the goal of optimising the bathroom experience and moving it away from the conservative world of sanitation products. In fact, Brian's economic knowledge has broadened Bathroom Mania!'s vision to also becoming among the first niched design studios focusing on sanitation ware.

The responses to the 'Kisses' urinal in particular were amazing and exceeded Meike and Brian's expectations, although manufacturers wavered on whether the daring approach could survive through the marketing process.

Certainly, the designs have remained illustrative and stimulating and it's particularly the surprises her works illicit that keep Meike passionately filling up those empty white spaces of the bathroom's interior.

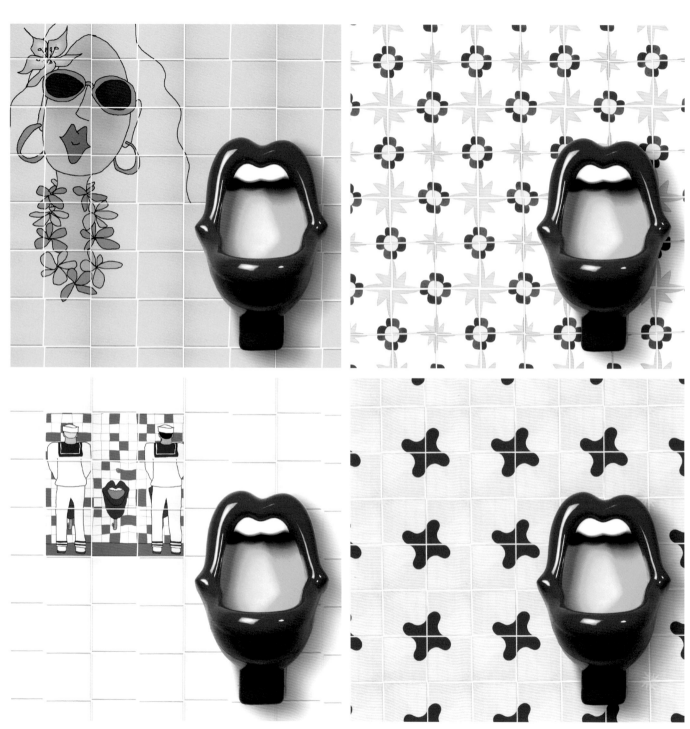

photography by / Bathroom-Mania • Meike

artist / Bathroom Mania! BV

location / The Netherlands

website / www.bathroom-mania.com

photography by / Jeroen Voolstra

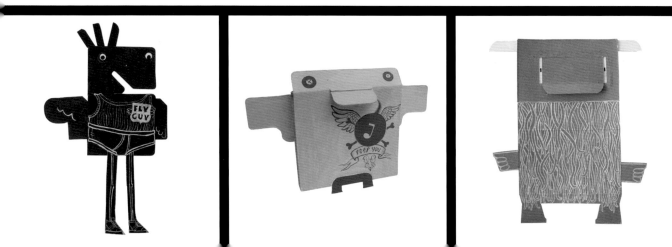

A "MUNICHAL" BOX:
BOX DOODLE PROJECT

www.boxdoodle.com

" It just popped into my mind some day when I received a package from a stock image agency. I unpacked the stuff — and then a nice shape of a box smiled at me from the top of my desk. I couldn't resist the smile, grabbed some markers from my desk, and started to doodle. "

– David Hofmann on his first box doodle –

His was originally an image of a cute character in white collared shirt, red tie and green buttons. More followed. All these have since then been virtually archived from February 2004. Today, David Hofmann's Box Doodle Project has also become an initiative to get people to see objects from a new angle.

The very first person he approached about the Box Doodle Project was Sune Ehlers of duudle.dk. The idea was well accepted by the public when one of his Hofmann's boxes appeared on the website. He thus continued with his approach, this time with a complete concept and proposal, to a few other sites including Design is Kinky, Netdiver and k10k. Since then, there has been an open invitation to anyone interested to have their box doodles published on his website for fun.

All this has reaped in some serious achievements. The Box Doodle Project was selected by the judges of D&AD as a record of great creativity for the year 2005. It has also been nominated for SOTY (Site of the Year) and was part of the shortlist of Netdiver's Best of the Year.

All this while being the creative director of an advertising agency in Munich has been challenging, if not demanding. Although Hofmann was born in Illinois, USA in 1971, most of his growing up years were spent in Southern Germany, where he later studied communication design in Munich.

His work since then has included creating successful campaigns for BMW and MINI for the European and Asian markets. In between tight deadlines, he is also a father to two little angels — Emily, 7 and Brenda, 15 — from his 14 years of marriage.

To him, there is always a place for creativity. And, it's nothing like a nice home by the lake in the south of Munich which allows him to be close to his family and nature, to foster it.

"I try to relax," says Hofmann. "To be playful and have fun has been my way to explore an idea. There are a lot of "creative techniques" to learn especially in advertising. But first of all, I have to be in a good mood."

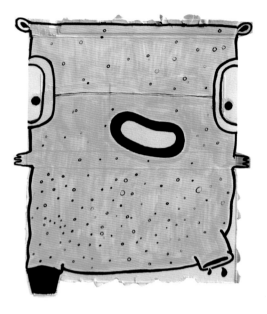

artist / Sarah Verroken

location / Wellington • New Zealand

website / www.sarahverroken.com

Vermelha Chair
photography by / Edra - Italy
Designed in 1993, it started being produced by Edra in 1998. The 500 meters of red rope are weaved by
hand creating the random looking loops. In reality there is structure method in the rather chaotic padding.

MAKING HEADLINES:
CAMPANAS

www.campanas.com.br

> "We play with all the materials that catch our attention. We see different possibilities of transforming and reshaping them. We try, each time more than before, to explore fewer materials that are environmentally incorrect."
>
> – Humberto and Fernando Campana –

Leather has undergone a revolution. In the hands of Sao Paolo-based Humberto and Fernando Campana, it's been used to swathe a chair to the effect of an unwanted animal whose coat has been left to grow in abandon. Yet, it's all deliberate. After all, the duo specialise in combining, using advanced manufacturing technologies, natural resources like wood, with found materials like rubber hose, ropes, plushies and fabric off-cuts.

Brazil's booming furniture industry and the market's demand for unique furniture has attracted many designers to step forward with several visually stimulating and sustainable products.

These include not least the Campana brothers. In their work, they often reinvent themselves conceptually while exemplifying the subject of transparency.

Humberto started out as a law practitioner, but then set up a small studio of sculptures. Fernando, who was a young architect by qualification, came forward in 1982 to give a helping hand. Besides the usual squabbles, they found each other pleasant to be around, and have since been able to maintain a strong sense of professionalism.

"We were born in the countryside of Sao Paolo state, in a city called Brotas (10,000 inhabitants), and when we were teens we moved to the capital (20,000,000 inhabitants). This sudden change provoked a cultural and transitional shock in us. How to decipher the differences of urban codes and signs has been our most precious learning experience."

Certainly, their craftsmanship has since been noticed by the public and a group of industry followers. Their furniture has been exhibited at gallery exhibitions in Sao Paolo (Casa Franca di Brasil), New York (Museum of Modern Art), London (Design Museum), Amsterdam (Extremely White) and Milan.

Masters of improvisation, Humberto and Fernando also have a part in education, teaching industrial design to students at Fundacao Alvares Penteado in Sao Paolo. In fact, they have come to consider the usage of their furniture itself potentially educational, allowing people to experience the reinvention of life's daily objects into furniture.

Anemone Chair

photography by / Edra - Italy
The Anemone chair is a Fernando and Humberto Campana design for Edra, produced since 2002 by the Italian company. This piece was born out of their constant research on new forms of seating.

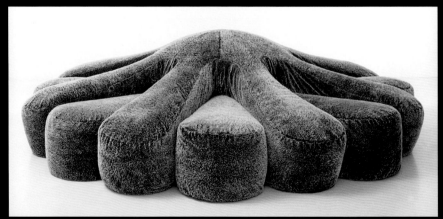

Historia Naturalis

photography by / Edra - Italy
Collection of sofas (Kaiman Jacaré and Aster Papposus) launched at the 2006 Salone in Milan. This is an evolution of the Boa Sofa, designed in 2002. Their idea was to "untie" the knots of Boa, proposing a modular and independent system of seats.

Here, Fernando and Humberto were exploring composable forms of seating. The organic shaped components can be freely assembled allowing a number of arrangements in its pieces.
Each arrangement transforms the aesthetics of the sofa making it new to the eye.

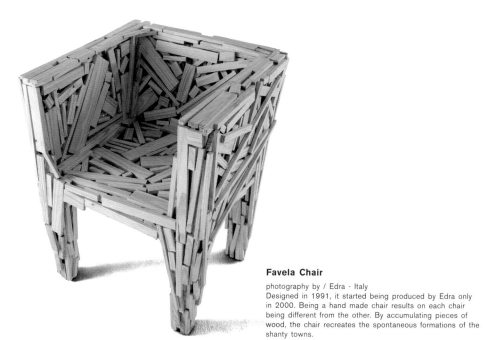

Favela Chair

photography by / Edra - Italy
Designed in 1991, it started being produced by Edra only in 2000. Being a hand made chair results on each chair being different from the other. By accumulating pieces of wood, the chair recreates the spontaneous formations of the shanty towns.

Estudo Campana Products / Banquete Chair

photography by / Luis Calazans
Designed in 2002, this chair plays with the idea of new forms of upholstery. It is an assemblage of stuffed animals arranged according to different sizes, colors, textures and heights in order to give balance to the piece.

artist / Carla Tennenbaum

location / São Paulo • Brazil

website / www.caobaum.com

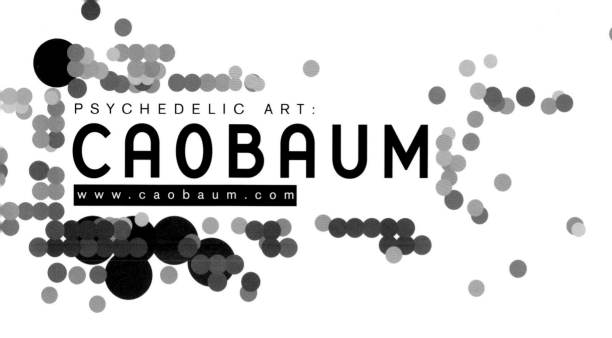

PSYCHEDELIC ART:
CAOBAUM
www.caobaum.com

> " I particularly enjoy working with paper refuse... and E.V.A for it's a material to which I've dedicated most of my attention so far, and which has allowed me to develop original techniques of revaluation. "
>
> – Carla Tennenbaum –

At university, design extraordinaire Carla Tennenbaum was a history major who always felt more of a fine artist. Well, what do you know, she was an artist. It wasn't long, in fact, before one of her works, the E.V.A wall tapestries won a prize at hOLAnDA 2003, stunning the Brazilian and international design scenes at the same time. It was just natural progression then, to move into industrial design, thus allowing her to create her personal artworks while incorporating within a playful attitude towards discarded materials.

In Sao Paulo, she lives in "an exciting and at the same time terrifying place where beauty and misery, opportunity and waste collide everywhere". Currently, she is handling a project known as EVAMARIA, through which she hopes to direct her creativity towards the "greater good" – making new art and design objects from discarded materials, and generating wage and respect for women excluded from the conventional job market.

The main purpose of her work has been to turn waste into opportunity, and refuse into value. She feels dejected that "the very nature of our sustained consumption patterns makes for the constant waste of valuable materials".

A few years ago, in fact, she designed an illustration for a Portuguese marketing agency, using a peculiar kind of refuse: tons of obsolete mobile phone accessories, produced in the 90s. She has also worked with rejected materials like old books, clothes, postcards, tin cans and wrappings.

The Kinetic Spirals, made from E.V.A (ethylene-vinyl-acetate) industrial refuse, is another of Carla's favourite creations. It took her years of hard work to perfect it and to create just the right mood for it. Ultimately, it has ended up the world's favourite.

"As far as I know, no one had used these techniques before, or made a chair out of crushed paper," says Carla. "Actually, I didn't even think of myself as a designer until a lot of people started calling me that."

Bursting into Brazil's design scene with ideas using eco-friendly materials, she is inspired by the wonderful sense of pleasure, the fragility of fine art, the rhythm of dance, the spontaneity of theatre, and the fluency of poetry. On a more personal note, she is influenced by the memory of her late grandmother Maria who was one of the wisest and most adorable people she'd met.

Besides ecological concern, Carla allows her craft to embrace a tongue-in-cheek style and a character of its own. "My work has a very strong visual impact, so recognition comes relatively fast in articles, exhibitions or prizes but the most important part has been fulfilling its potential for positive ecological and social impact from an artist's point of view," says Carla.

artist / Carla Tennenbaum

location / São Paulo • Brazil

website / www.caobaum.com

CRAFTING VALUES:
CARTER WONG TOMLIN

www.carterwongtomlin.com

" We like to play around with ideas in our work that challenge the brief. We've always believed in simple clear solutions as well, and something that won't date easily, so we don't tend to go for a stylish approach to our work, rather more pared down. We enjoy pushing the boundaries though; right through to the printing and production of a job, experimenting with materials and finishes when possible. "

– Carter Wong Tomlin –

Phil Carter and Phil Wong pursued the same degree course at Norwich School of Art followed by a further three years at the Royal College of Art where they studied for their Master of Arts, Royal College of Art (MARCA). Not only sharing a name and the same dreams in the same competitive industry, they also shared a friendship which helped them set up their own agency in 1984, Carter Wong Tomlin, with the addition of Ali Tomlin as fellow director.

Since then, they have created designs for fast-moving consumer goods such as Deberdt Chocolate, Bombay Emporium, Unilever and Waitrose as well as advertising campaigns for Boden, Howies and Lloyd's. It has been the success of campaigns such as the one for Wall's ice cream and the prestigious F1 logo

however, that have earned Carter Wong Tomlin recognition as gurus in advertising and branding.

Although one could imagine that each designer ought to find a niche to stick their teeth into and just do it, their approach to design is very personal as each client is inimitable and deserves a finished project that reflects them and only them.

"We are unique in that we have the mix of Wong's Eastern influences, coupled with my own Western values," says Carter.

Let's also not forget just the fundamental thrill that the both of them still get from a constant visual awareness that ultimately and inevitably rubs off on their work. "I am me in the way I design because

of the continual fascination I have for visual things, from the endless books I buy and paintings, to 'finds' at flea markets to drawing every day and taking photographs of subjects that interest me."

The design scene in London is, as ever, constantly changing with new start-ups emerging every week. Rather than competing, Phil Carter would like to think of these newcomers as complementing their work and giving clients more options for their marketing budgets, so that complacency is less likely to creep in.

Besides design, another personal passion includes cycling, an outdoor activity which frees the partner of this award-winning company from work and worries.

OF FOLKLORE AND LEGENDS:
CATALINA
ESTRADA

www.catalinaestrada.com

> 66 I love to see illustrations when they become alive in fashion, 3D objects and even as displays on the streets of Barcelona. 99
>
> – Catalina Estrada –

Catalina Estrada was born and raised in Colombia in the company of extravagant nature, legends and century-old folklore. In 1999 however, she moved to Barcelona, Spain, bringing with her the unbreakable spirit of the children she helped to aid back in her homeland. Her little friends represented a turning point in her career path as they inspired her to create a rainbow of dreamy effects fused with Latin-American folklore, and bright and glowing images filled with hope, love, colour and as always, life.

Her symmetrical, well-composed illustrations bear a lot of significance to her family and the place she grew up in and loved all these years. The intricate patterns and strokes of her drawings are a picture of nature borne from her childhood experience, familiarity and intimacy with colours. Catalina is also very much into art nouveau, modernism, the arts and crafts movement and Latin American art. Her illustrations are a culmination of wild imaginations – emotive and expressive.

She finds her art the only gentle way to suppress her angst against worldly issues (injustice, child abuse, etc.). She sees realism as something that people would "feel" when they come across these images.

Catalina's series of illustrations have travelled across continents and into countries as far and wide as UK, Barcelona, Germany, Spain, Australia and Japan. The freelance illustrator's clients include Coca-Cola, Paul Smith, Nike, Honda, Custo-Barcelona, Salomon, Chronicle Books and others.

Of late, Catalina has been in a collaborative mood teaming up with a couple of fashion labels. A few of her vivid designs and embroideries have been dressing up clothes from Brazilian's Anunciaçao.

Most of all however, the graduate in Fine Arts (lithography major) and Plastic Arts is the happiest when she has all the freedom to create and dwell in a sphere where fantasy begets fantasy, in the comfort of her home.

photography by / Fernanda Calfat

00 / Coca-cola Poster Design &
Coca-cola Limited Edition Bottle
(Eastern Campaign, Australia)

CATALINA ESTRADA
PATROCINA   1ª MOSTRA INTERNACIONAL D'ART URBÀ PUBLICITARI

Nightology. by
www.jbnightology.com

MURO

International Outdoor Urban Art Exhibition
sponsored by J&B. 10 selected artists create specific artworks
to be exposed in 44 giant billboards across streets of Barce

00 / Catalina Estrada for Paul Smith
Autum / Winter 2007 collection

00 / Catalina Estrada for Paul Smith
Showroom Display

artist / Takeshi Nakamura / Yuichi Kodama / Yusuke Tanaka

location / Tokyo • Japan

website / www.caviar.ws

SOFT CREAM

stuffz ▼ 080 • 081 ▲

art direction by / Yusuke Tanaka
photography by / Mayumi Koshiishi
H/M by / Asami Nemoto
stylist by / Kiyomi Yoshihara

DRIVING TOKYO'S MOTION GRAPHIC SCENE:

CAVIAR

www.caviar.ws

> " Caviar consists of 10 people who worked at a record company, worked at an ad agency, was mad about gambling, has lived in Columbia, and was a Chemistry major at a university. Yeah, everyone from Caviar has a different story to tell. "

– Takeshi Nakamura, Caviar Limited –

Founded by Takeshi Nakamura in 2000, Caviar Limited has been titillating audiences with its promotional films, edgy music videos and animations. In 2007, it was listed as one of 100 leading Japanese Motion Graphic Creators.

With its strong roster of directors and computer graphics creators, Caviar has produced several notable films, such as Runnnnner, a stop-motion animation directed by Nakamura, and a bottle design for Coke with elements taken from Caviar's other film, Milky Way.

Besides short films, they are known to produce well thought-out commercials, DVDs and award-winning music videos. The video for the song "I My Me Mine",

directed by Yuichi Kodama, for example, won Best Concept Video at the 2006 Space Shower Music Video Awards. The next year, Yuichi won the coveted Best New Artist Video Award for his brilliant visual execution of Base Ball Bear's fast-paced "Electric Summer".

While most directors in Japan find their niche in either commercials or music videos, Caviar prefers to work in both categories. In a way, Kodama says that Caviar's spin on the trade is to include something out-of-the-ordinary in their visuals to attract more viewers, and that the best ideas usually become visible at the very last minute.

artist / Takeshi Nakamura / Yuichi Kodama / Yusuke Tanaka

location / Tokyo • Japan

website / www.caviar.ws

design by / Takeshi Nakamura
website / www.clubking.com

design by / Takeshi Nakamura / Misa Nakamura
website / www.clubking.com

design by / Yusuke Tanaka
website / www.uno-caol-showten.com   00 / T-shirts Design

artist / Takeshi Nakamura / Yuichi Kodama / Yusuke Tanaka

location / Tokyo • Japan

website / www.caviar.ws

design by / Takeshi Nakamura

art direction / Takeshi Nakamura

00 / Hanging Light Design

THE CLASSICS HAVE A NAME:

CHARMING UNIT

www.charmingunit.com

> " My favourite materials are paper and cardboard. I use them to build prototypes and they're fantastic. "
>
> – Louise Hederström, Charming Unit Design Studio –

Charming Unit Design Studio from Malmö, Sweden's third largest city, has been driven creatively by Louise Hederström since 2005. Before this, Louise studied at Beckmans School of Design, obtained a working scholarship at IKEA, and also worked at the office of Swedish industrial and graphic designer Björn Dahlströms.

Going back a bit more, Louise grew up on a farm in the south of Sweden. As the youngest among her siblings, she filled up most of her time with knitting, sewing and doing carpentry as well as other handiwork.

"Maybe it sounds weird to say this but I still feel that my interest in doing all these started out of boredom," says Louise whose idol is the late King of Rock and Roll, Elvis Presley. The iconic personality has been an inspiration to her since she was four years old. The furniture designer is very much attached to the times of 1968 to 1972 when music, clothes and stage design were marvelous.

"Arts and crafts, new materials, new techniques and of course, nature is also of great importance to me. I just love those moments when you get an idea that you have belief in and think is very good to be applied onto design."

She shares the example of an ordinary chair created with good design: "Everybody wants to make a chair but a few manage to get it right. I'm more interested in finding a unique solution when I work with different materials and functions. For me, I will give the chair a graphic shape that is sustainable and adds more value to the product itself."

Specifically, her works include the Scatter for Nola and the Arild seats for NC Möbler, as well as amazing space interiors prepared for furniture exhibitions in Milano and Stockholm during the past years. With the help of her husband, a designer too, she managed to pull off a series of lacy and extravagant Gladys Chandeliers for Belysningsbolaget. Charming Unit has also done commissioned works for Tetra Pak, Ericsson and IKEA in addition to Scandinaviaform and Maze International.

Exhibition Milan 04 is together with Maxjenny Forslund who designed the sofa and Elin Forslund who designed the glass lamps on the wall.

01
02

01 / Hanging Lamp Design
02 / Exhibition Milan 04

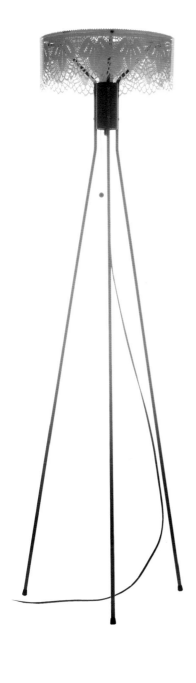

Stockholm 05 at Wetterling Gallery together with Möbelmössan ("Furniture Cap").

00 / Standing Light Design

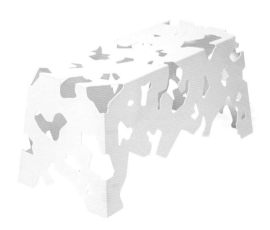

artist / Nicola Carter / Luise Vormittag

location / Germany

website / www.containerplus.co.uk

photography by / Jenny Nordquis

00 / Virtue - Personal Project

CONTAINER

www.containerplus.co.uk

> " Illustration is becoming installation is becoming performance is becoming photography is becoming theatre is becoming art is becoming music is becoming happening. "
>
> – Container –

Beyond sketches, painting and illustrations lie a whole new chapter filled with challenges, odds and the occasional temperament as partners of Container, Nicola Carter and Luise Vormittag continue to work hand in hand designing. For three years and counting, the pair have learned to come to terms with their ability to create beautiful things that people adore.

"Not every piece can be endued with personal ideas and emotions," explains one of them, adding that working in this line is an uphill struggle. When one of them needed a rest, the other one would plough on. It goes to say that some works emerge from a playful approach with materials, lucky accidents or the necessity to pay the bills.

From time to time, the graduates, who both took up a major in Graphic Design from London's Camberwell College of Art, make fun of themselves through their illustrations, wall paintings, installations and interior design. They rave over the insanity of the design world, making the impossible possible.

"My impression is that people in the creative communities are becoming increas-

ingly fluid in regards to boundaries," says Nicole. Whatever that means, it means the designers now brave the odds and fully work out their imagination.

Recently, Container teamed up with Simon Husslein to build the first Haunted House in Hamburg, Germany – the kind of exhibition filled with gothic elements and tells the story about Container.

Along the line, the multi-disciplinary art and design partnership based in East London has explored various media commissioned by Volkswagen and Hotel Fox, Becks, Olay, Selfridges, Sanrio and publications such as Computer Arts Magazine, Elle Girl, MTV and Channel 5.

Strange as it may sound, Nicola and Luise see things on the brighter side because they believe that Container is "born out of the collective clutter of their minds, like a storm in a teacup, dark dreams of spilled ink, some dolls house furniture and ridiculous gossips passed on with suppressed laughter."

client / Bitburger
time / January 2006
location /
Bread and Butter fashion fair, Berlin, Germany
type of work /
Live art event - we painted the backdrop of the fair during
the 3 days of the event
photography by / Mario Priske

description /
Bitburger decided to launch their new drink "Passion" at the
BBB fair. Container were commissioned to come up with
their own interpretation of "Passion" and apply it to the 15m
long wall during the 3 days of the fair.

We worked in mixed media: some sections were prepard in
London and brought to Berlin as printouts, that were then
cut out and attached to the wall, other areas were painted
there and some sections filled with wallpaper.

00 / Backdrop for Bitburger
Passion Lounge at BBB

client / Volkswagen, Germany
time / Christmas 2005
type of work /
Design of christmas stationary, giftbox and baubles
for VW

description /
Container were commissioned to design the christmas
greeting card and envelope for Volkswagen. Alongside
the stationary we also were asked to create a gift box
for an assortment of chocolates, as well as circular
designs which were inserted into transparent baubles
and were used as decoration for wreaths.

We worked the circular design of the baubles into the
entire range: the circles povide different characters a
secure environment for
hibernation.

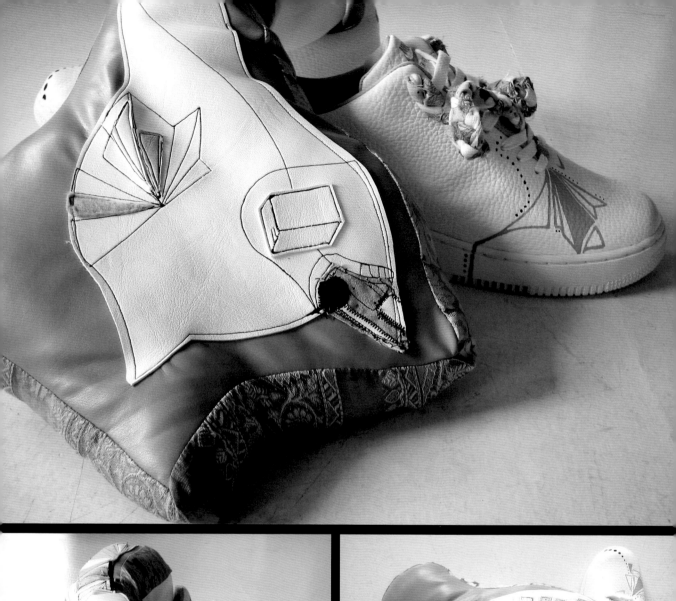

artist / Nicola Carter / Luise Vormittag

location / Germany

website / www.containerplus.co.uk

client / Elle Girl / Hachette Filipacchi UK
time / January 2005
location / London
type of work /
Painted backdrop for fashion shoot.
copywrite by / Container and Anna Rosa Krau

description /
Container were commissioned to produce a backdrop for the
shoot.The work was carried out in close
collaboration with the fashion photographer Anna Rosa Krau.
Published in issue 24, April 2005 Elle Girl UK.

links /
http://www.annarosa.com

SPACE FOR THOUGHT:
CRINSON
www.crinson.com

66
Balance the hi-tech with the spiritual, the natural with the ornate, and the playful with the stylish.
99

– Dominic Crinson –

London-based Dominic Crinson designs 100% recyclable, made-to-order tiles and wallpapers which are all about richness in quality and classic beauty. Merging high technology with ornate designs, which are something of a Dominic Crinson trademark, his recent showcase of the latest in tiles and wallpapers at the London Design Festival was inspired by an assortment of colours such as grey, gold and strawberry red, combined with metallic and textured glass overlays.

Colours when matched harmoniously result in desired effects and Crinson seems to have mastered this technique. In 2006 he won the coveted title "Designers' Choice Best Designer Award 2006" at the Seoul Living Design Fair in Tokyo. Seoul could get much more of Dominic since he opened a boutique showroom in Seo-cho, downtown Seoul, in the same year.

Focusing on shapes and shades attained through the use of high technology and digitally processed images, Dominic's style has been described as appealing equally to domestic decorators, expressive designers, cruiseship operators and international hoteliers. His clients include Park Hotel in New Delhi as well as Bombay Sapphire, which commissioned him to design a range of tiles called "Complexity" with inspirations drawn from the North African and Far Eastern regions.

Not surprisingly, Dominic has received a fair share of press. Australia's interior magazine Inside Out, for one, has gushed about his "striking, colourful and supremely covetable" masterpieces.

 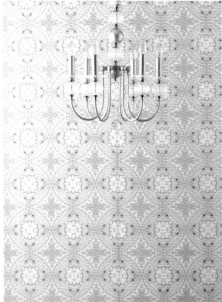 

MADE TO MEASURE:
DEIN DESIGN
www.dein-design.com

> 66 Personally, we definitely try to keep the standard high but customers' tastes are always important. We have a good balance in providing designs our customers request and designs that are important to us as well. 99
>
> – Dein Design –

In Germany, things are going great for Dein Design and Co. This successful business producing printed vinyl foils for electronic devices such as laptops, turntables, tattooing machines as well as furniture, Dein Design has in its collection a wide range of designs made to measure for every individual needs.

On how the brilliant idea crossed his mind, Kyan Noack says everything started with music and originated from there. "That was the reason for a longer stay in London in the middle of 2005," says Noack, the managing director of Dein Design. "I had to get myself a notebook to be able to work properly but after three months of using it, (I was bored by the look of it) so I decided to make it special."

Back in Germany, the enterprising lad talked to his brother about the idea. Then, they realised that other people are also interested in designing their electronic devices in a style they like.

Since then, Dein Design has been working with designers from around the world, and not limited to, Felix Kiessling (London), Beatrize Isaura Cantú Brandi (Mexico), Niko Stumpo (Amsterdam), Scotty76 and Timo Würz (Germany), Ndeur (Toronto), YABA and TVboy (Barcelona) to name a few.

These collaborative exchanges between the company and the designers are ongoing. Dein Design establishes a network of creative artists far beyond graphic and design. Customers, too, can be their own designers.

"It's awesome to see customers being creative and sending in their own individual designs," says Noack. "There are boundless opportunities for everybody out there to express themselves in unique ways."

If it is signing up designers for an upcoming project, Noack looks for a design that's relevant to what DesignSkins requires. Technically speaking, Dein Design provides high quality vinyl foils printed ac-

curately to size and applicable to electronic devices and furniture.

"We want to give people the opportunity to be individualistic, artistic, different, independent, expressive, innovative, creative, fashionable and therefore, beautiful."

For example, Dein Design cooperates with music artists or music festivals, providing a perfect merchandise for their music contents. DesignSkins, the brand of Dein Design's printed vinyl foils, is "more like a platform than just a nice product" which aims to communicate visually and bridge people with design.

Besides that, Noack feels it's also important to work with motivated designers with good communication skills. Though the company is in a convenient position to choose works from a bunch of designers, Noack is forward-looking that there are more talents out there on the streets still waiting for an opportunity to impact the design world.

artist / Kyan Noack

location / Germany

website / www.dein-design.com

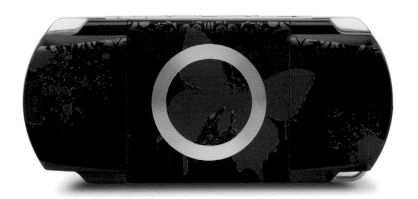

01 / Mobile Phone Skin Design
02 / i-Pod Skin Design
03 / i-Pod Shuffle Skin Design

artist / Delaware

location / Tokyo • Japan

website / www.de.bc.re.gr.jp

"Dokuro"
Men's Fashion Trade Fair, Pitti Uomo.
Fortezza Da Basso, Florence. 2003.

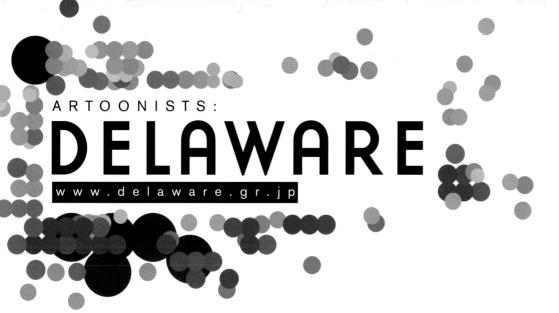

ARTOONISTS:
DELAWARE
www.delaware.gr.jp

" The difference is not between the original
or the remix version and the audio equipment
used in making the music. It's those experiences in
life that make a familiar piece of music sound
different from one person to another. As I get older,
my James Brown starts to sound different too. "

– Delaware –

The Japanese super sonic group, Delaware, has been storming the streets with their creative abilities. These "artoonists" (the word is derived from the words cartoon and art) not only make music but Bitmap art. Proud members of this gung-ho group are Masato Samata, Aya Honda and Morihiro Tajiri.

Samata founded Delaware in 1993 and discovered brilliant talents like Honda and Tajiri who joined forces two years later. The group then grew bigger with the addition of Ten in 1997 and Yoshiki Watanabe in 2002 who both left the association in 2001 and 2007 respectively.

They make everything from music to magazines, recordings, visual installations, writing, web design, mobile phone art, posters, cross stitch and, of course, live performances of their electrifying music. Artoons for music? It is decidedly so.

Bitmaps appear to be the right technique for these guys. Quoting Delaware in its website, bitmap images, though working with squares and offering confined movement, is as simple as Lego and at the same time, a merit to the person who makes it work.

Delaware believes in fusing music with art and cartoons in illustrative bitmaps. They have had several live shows at New York's ARTOON at P.S.1 (2001), Barcelona's Japan Graphics (2002), Hong Kong's IDN/ My Favourite Conference (2002) and Paris' D-Day Design Today (2005). They have also contributed to and released several CD compilations including Surfin' USSR, With the Delaware, Delaware Strikes Back and AmeN.

When it comes to 'designing' their music, Samata dedicates himself to composition, vocals, text editing and art direction. Honda lays his fingers on the bass guitar while Tajiri rocks the stage with the drums. Watanabe meanwhile, explores sound programming and ringer phone compositions.

"Birth Of Venus"
Men's Fashion Trade Fair, Pitti Uomo.
Fortezza Da Basso, Florence. 2003.

"You Made Bank. I Made Pyram
Book, Design In The Rain.
publisher / Actor, Barcelona. 2004

"Sneakers Stitch"
Cross S+I+CH. VANS sneakers. 2005

01
02

01 / 'We Are Small' Design
02 / 'Singin' Small' Design

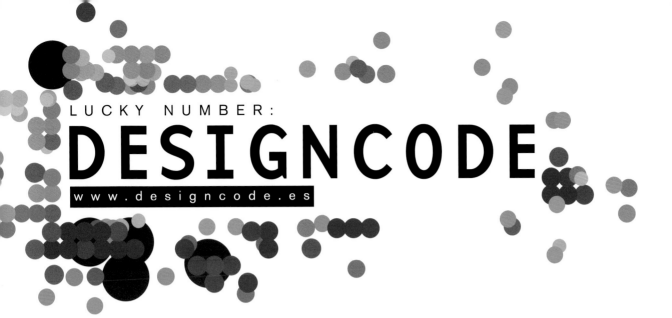

LUCKY NUMBER:
DESIGNCODE
www.designcode.es

66 What motivates us each new day is to consider that we promote take-away Design: sensational design within the reach of everyone. 99

– Design Code –

Spanish-based DesignCode introduced Flamps to the market at Maison & Objet in September 2007. Along with Japanese leading designer Hiroshi Tsunoda, they also came out with campaigns and designs such as the BCN Lamp, Bits Vivid, Orbit Mini, Big Cleopatra, La Fortune, Fleep and Joyn, not to mention the option of having a bit of Barcelona sun shining on your table.

Barcelona-based Tsunoda meanwhile, has built an industrial empire of his own in this foreign country. When it comes to personalising a campaign, he creates new objects with the following characteristics: functional, practical and sensational.

Many clients or companies from different sectors have benefited from the creativity of DesignCode. They include Hewlett-Packard, SEAT, Vincon, Desigual, Hesperia Tower, InfoJobs.net, Melnik, Barrio Santo, Aquipo Singular, Vasava, Small Back Room, Freshthink, Small and Attitude.

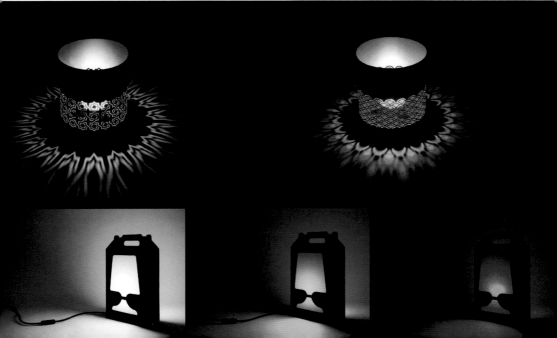

artists / Steffen Sauerteig / Svend Smital / Kai Vermehr

location / Berlin • Germany

website / www.eboy.com

PIXEL FAIR:
EBOY
www.eboy.com

> ❝ Our daily work is to make pictures and we use the computer only to do this. All we do is virtual, but we like the warmth of wood, heaviness of metal and broad variety of plastics. ❞
>
> – eBoy –

The people behind eBoy have been generating extensive media attention for their pixel art. Because of them, Nike, Coca-Cola, Honda, MTV and even household consumer goods like Kellogg's have surrendered to the hype of their Legoesque virtual world. The public can't get enough of them, either. So, the world is crazy about eBoy. They've been getting publicity and commissioned works from numerous magazines and corporate companies since their startup in 1998. Before that however, Steffen Sauerteig, Kai Vermehr and Svend Smital had a track record of 9 years in the business together in Berlin, Germany.

Steffen began his working life as an electrician and went on to build sets for East German television. He studied visual communication at the College of Fine Art in Berlin from 1991-96 before joining eBoy. Svend was born in 1967 the same year as Steffen, trained as a bricklayer from 1984 to1987 and later graduated from the Berlin Academy of Art in 1996. The third member of eBoy, Kai grew up in Frankfurt am Main in Germany and spent his childhood days in Guatemala. He obtained a qualification for communication design from Folkswangschule in Essen and down the road, even released two LP records.

Certainly, at this point in the variegated path that they've trodden, whatever they are doing now is done for the love of design.

"That's not about imparting emotions but taking care of every detail that defines the quality of our work," says eBoy with an understanding that the design scene is a crazy universe, humbly admitting that they know only a tiny part of it, most of which is otherwise not applicable to them.

They believe that this universe is not made up of any one design scene but a community of designers who wants a piece of the cake and constantly grows bigger than before.

They add: "We don't intend to differentiate ourselves. It just happens. Maybe how we work is kind of unique since we share all of our work between the three of us. This way our pictures get more value and are richer in design than one single person could ever achieve. This is no child's play as each design goes through a tedious process to get the three-dimensional effect." Perhaps their past experience laying bricks or making up electrical circuits helps though, and as many and certainly eBoy's fans would testify, it's all worth it.

01 / Plate Design
02 / Levi's T-shirt Design
03 / Stickers Design
04 / CD Design
05 / Pepsi Bottle's Label Design

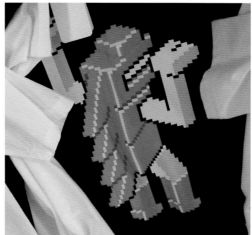

00 / Eboy for Paul Smith Design

Letterbox painting for STAMP, Orchard Road, Singapore.

EESHAUN

www.eeshaun.com

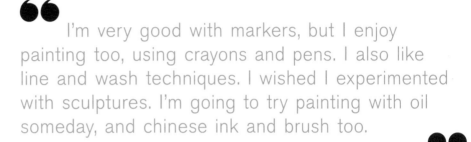

" I'm very good with markers, but I enjoy painting too, using crayons and pens. I also like line and wash techniques. I wished I experimented with sculptures. I'm going to try painting with oil someday, and chinese ink and brush too. "

– Eeshaun –

Eeshaun's Gardensilly website was put up on the Internet after the lad graduated from the School of Communication and Information in Nanyang Technological University, Singapore, in 2005. He viewed it as a means of provoking the island state's public on its education system, startling viewers on its opening page with the confrontational question "Are you silly?"

The self-trained illustrator comes to terms with accepting doodling as not just a hobby but a career which he may excel in. Sure enough, the design scene in Singapore is dynamic with several furniture makers, interior designers, graphic designers and artists at hand to satisfy a demand for well-thought out designs. It is seemingly competitive with almost no space to grow.

The time has been right for Eeshaun however and he has found a unique style which allows him to stand out from the rest.

To date, Eeshaun has created illustrations for STAMP SG, Tagger Bag, Gokitsch, Local Brand, Territory (HK), FARM, Play Imaginative, IDN and Tiger Translate-Rise. His works have also been exhibited at Cardboard Art Exhibition (2007), Street Art Manila Expo (2006), CLEO Fashion

Awards (2006) and IDN Design Edge (2005). The 26-year-old also contributed 'Fat Snap Cats' for the 100 Chairs Project, organised by the National Youth Council for the Children's Society.

While he usually gives in to procrastination, he enjoys the bursts of energy and whimsical ideas which come from the interaction between his inner soul and society at large.

"It's the freedom in art that I love. I've been drawing all my life as a hobby, but I never took it seriously," says Eeshaun with a rather focussed tone which suggests that he is now sinking his teeth into design for some time to come.

"I like to create drawings that are spontaneous and to make up creatures and characters, as I'm big on improvisation," he says. To him, each piece is unique and drawn with a diffcrence and if it doesn't make him laugh in any way, then it isn't a good piece at all. Indeed, one person Eeshaun constantly challenges with the question "Are you silly?" must surely be himself.

SINGPOST POSTAGE RATES
EFFECTIVE 18 DECEMBER 2006

Place envelope below to check if it is ISO standard size.

C4

Letterbox painting for STAMP, Orchard Road, Singapore.

Marker on fiberglass, lamp made from khong guan biscuit can mold.
for sale at maad market, red dot design museum, Singapore

Customization for Tagger messenger bags from Holland, for sale at Vivocity, Singapore.

Contribution to 100 chairs, non-profit chair painting art exhibition organised by national youth council and nanyang technological university. proceeds go to children's society, 2007.

DESIGNERS FROM MADRID:

EL ULTIMO GRITO

www.elultimogrito.co.uk

"Together, their network of national and international clients are proof that El Ultimo Grito is a creative studio which excels in design produced in many forms."

– El Ultimo Grito –

In 1997, Spanish designers Roberto Feo and Rosario Hurtado earned The Blueprint Design Award at 100% Design in London for their Miss Ramirez Chair. They repeated this coup the following two years with their Mind the Gap coffee table and Good Morning Moneypenny self-assembled coat hanger.

Formed in 1997 by Robert and Rosario along with former partner Francisco Santos, the studio started manufacturing their own products with a collection entitled Minimal Maximum, which attempted to create maximum results using the minimum of materials.

Robert was born in London in 1964 and had grown up in Madrid. There he studied sociology in the capital's Complutense University but moved back to London in 1990 to study furniture design at the London College of Furniture. He then gleaned a Master of Arts (MA) in Furniture Design from the prestigious Royal Academy of Art. In 1997, he founded El Ultimo Grito with partner Rosario Hurtado.

Rosario had been a student of Economics at the Alcala de Henares University in Madrid before moving to London in 1989. There she studied Cabinet Making and Furniture Design at the London College of Furniture and completed her Bachelor of Arts (BA) in Industrial Design at Kington University.

Together, their network of national and international clients are proof that El Ultimo Grito is a creative studio which excels in design produced in many forms. Their clients are mainly from the UK (Marks & Spencer, Joinedupdesignforschools, Mathmos, Griffin, Bloomberg, Wireworks), Spain (Orden en Casa, Punt Mobies), Italy (Magis, Abet laminate, Lavazza) and Japan (E&Y, Style).

The studio also emphasises installations in between commissioned projects. Several of their works have been exhibited at the UK's Manchester Art Galleries, Victoria & Albert Museum, Crafts Council, British Council and Science Museum.

Roberto and Rosario have also been featured in print publications such as Designers on Design, Collydoscope, International Design Yearbook 2004, Extracity and Spoon.

2006 'Tagged #6' at Stanley Picker Gallery
Installation transforming space using discarded materials
found on the galleries vicinity and then rendered with
specially design stickers.

2006 'Tagged #6' at Stanley Picker Gallery
Installation transforming space using discarded materials
found on the galleries vicinity and then rendered with
specially design stickers.

2001 the Funktion Object (self production)
rotomoulded polyethelene.
Modular object which as single piece can act as stool,
when combined can be use to generate different
furniture solutions both for children and adults

2005 West London Academy primary school area
'Theatre / playground / table' hand painted fibre
glass 25sqm table where you can go in for theatre
plays and sits a class around.
'Shelve space divider'

00 / Installation Art

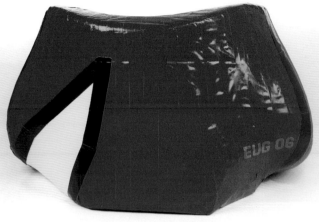

artist / Roberto Feo / Rosario Hurtado

location / Spanish

website / www.elultimogrito.co.uk

'Tape Chairs' & 'Tape sofa'
2006 single polyurethane bed mattress and cardboard,
binded / upholstered with tape.

Macros 2007

'Girafas' domestic lamppost
'Mass' light/sitting public piece
one-off pieces made from
reclaimed materials

2004 Land Ho for Nola (Sweden)
public sitting / planter in roto
moulded polyethelene

Ipso Crafto 2007
'Bench to Bench' soft to hard
bench mutation
'Hump' bench mutation

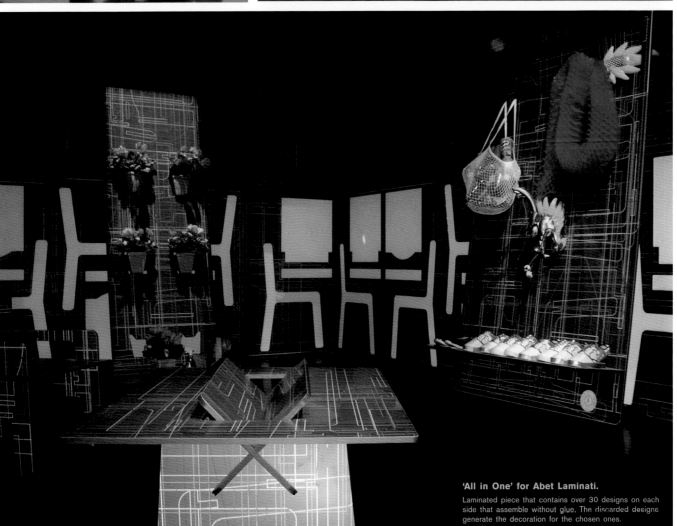

'All in One' for Abet Laminati.

Laminated piece that contains over 30 designs on each
side that assemble without glue. The discarded designs
generate the decoration for the chosen ones.

artist / Roberto Feo / Rosario Hurtado

location / Spanish

website / www.elultimogrito.co.uk

artist / Roberto Feo / Rosario Hurtado

location / Spanish

website / www.elultimogrito.co.uk

2001 Griffin Shop / Portobello, London
Shop conceived as a walking ward rove, the only thing that exist is a system of hooks in the ceiling and the shop changes continuesly by installations

2004 'GauDiY @ Elisava (tagged environments)
Students area generated using thrown away material found around the school and rendered with especially design sticker which suggests Gaudi's mosaic

01 / Boutique Display
02 / 2004 'GauDiY @ Elisava

Selfridges Window for Griffin 2003 • tagged environments

2005 Griffin Soho • tagged environments
Ephemeral show room in Carnaby Street, London. Generated with all the packing material thrown away by neighbouring business. Rendered with white computer stickers

00 / Cans Design

YOUNG AND REBELLIOUS:
EXTRAVERAGE
www.extraverage.net

" Pencils and markers were always my tool until my father got our first computer. That was when it changed, and it's been my passion ever since. "

– Karoly Kiralyfalvi, founder of drezign.hu –

Budapest, Hungary, is home to graphic designer Karoly Kiralyfalvi. At a very young age, he was taught by his father about techniques in painting. Today, he hasn't reached his late 20s, but he has probably seen and learned more about design than those older may have gained in a school, and knows how to use it to manipulate one's thoughts.

As a nasty little boy who loved to draw and build blocks of legos, Karoly never skipped art classes and would always doodle anything that came to mind on his drawing block. His father, meanwhile, was the perfect combination of a painter, poet and sculptor, who passed down his craftsmanship to his son.

In 2001, Karoly started his first job at a studio called Solid. Having practiced drawing for many years, he kept learning and found a focus in computer graphics and vector-based software. He served as an operator and graphic designer for several teams in the past four to five years before creating his own brand, Drezign.

Drezign holds on to the influences and inspirations received from his past ex-

periences – from the music he's heard, magazines he's bought and websites he's viewed to the books he's particularly liked.

In 2001, Karoly got actively involved in Hungary's street art scene. He's also ventured into mixed media such as custom spraycans, shoes, skateboard decks, T-shirts, posters and wallpapers.

With all the media coverage, reviews and support from reputable publications, Karoly is now hard to miss. His logos were featured in the book Graphicum, published by the Society of Hungarian Graphic Designers And Typographers, while the rest of his illustrations have been featured in UK's Digital Arts, Computer Arts and Blowback magazines.

His other works have also been featured in World Wide Connections PDF Magazine, the new Print4Street urban art gallery, WOW! Cartoon and Comic Auction Showcase, Castro Restobar Showcase, You Are Beautiful Book Project, Play Loud! Book Feature and limited edition designs for Logik Clothing.

Carhartt Installation Art

artist / Karoly Kiralyfalvi

location / Budapest • Hungary • Europe

website / www.extraverage.net / www.drezign.hu / www.logikwear.com

adidas x extraverage™

thisaintnohalfsteppin

adidas x extraverage™

superstar

00 / Shluffyfox Design

" We've worked with plush, metal sculptures, food, fiberglass, computer, video, etc. We never limit our creativity to anything. Like, if we want to build a ladder to heaven, it might be best to make it inflatable rather than from a piece of wood because we can reach higher with it now. "

– FriendsWithYou –

The effervescent Miami-based team of Friendswithyou (FWY) presents art and toys together and –wham!– creates a bagful of magic in the process. Sam Borkson (Sam) and Arturo Sandoval (Tury) are on the hunt for more animated friends to join their group of irresistible plushies and to help grow a huge following. FWY sews the toys singlehandedly whilst casting magic on them so that they become the friendliest aliens around.

Sam and Tury's witty personalities are pleasantly reflected in the grand storyline of FWY. Since its inception in 2002, Sam and Tury have also been working harder than ever to achieve the passport to everyone's heart with their characters.

In the midst of a magical garden, where all the birds fly and little kids play hide and seek, Friendswithyou are managed by these two dynamic adults who always push themselves forward to go beyond

their comfortable accomplishments and reach for the stars. While Tury works on impending projects, Sam tosses around with their Malfis –a bizarre take on what's cuddly– in the studio.

Throughout the years as a team, the boys have pondered on their self-carved niche in this world and what to do with their talent. In terms of opportunity, they have had invitations from interested parties wanting them to apply their creativity onto platforms including, but not limited to, playgrounds, fashion apparel, stationery, furniture and home decor, art prints and publications, muiltimedia and entertainment.

Certainly, Sam and Tury have forayed into their fair share of media, including a series of art installations and exhibitions, such as the Cloud City installation and performance at Art Basel (2005), Fertility Shrine, Harmony's

Helm, King Albino Room Heavenly Palace, Albino Fox Car for Project Fox Hotel (2005), Skywalkers blimp parade at Art Basel (2006), Rainbow Valley playground installation at Aventura Mall (2006), and the Wish Come True sculpture series at Galerie Emmanuel Perrotin (May 2007).

There have also been merchandising and commercial projects with big organisations like MTV, VH1, Nickelodeon, Comedy Central, Nike, Volkswagen, Toyota Scion, Redbull, Target, Sony, BMW, Mini Cooper, And1, Hasbro and Vitamin Water.

Walking the design line has never been easy but it's worth embracing every minute of it with the ever-growing community of FWY characters. They enjoy learning from successes and even more from failures, but most of all, they enjoy the adventure more than anything else.

Photography by / Sebastian Gray

00 / Hotels Installation Design

00 / Rainbow Valley Installation Design

artist / Friends With You

website / www.friendswithyou.com

artist / Ryosuke Tei

location / Japan

website / www.furifuri.com

00 / FATBEAR Series Memory Stick

CARTOON MADNESS:
FURI FURI
www.furifuri.com

"Furi Furi characters are akin to radical figures from past Japanese comics in terms of colours and animated features."

– Furi Furi –

Tokyo-based Furi Furi Company, headed by Ryosuke Tei, is one of Japan's top design houses focusing on excessive cuteness in both appeal and character. Right from their first animated creation, Electronic Virus, the attention of toy collectors was attracted. Nine years after its initiation in 1998, Furi Furi now stands a notch above the rest.

Ryosuke was born in Osaka to a Chinese father and a Japanese mother and graduated from Tama Art University. Half of his formative years were spent travelling throughout Asia to better understand his mixed identity. The work he has done for Furi Furi since then reflects this continuing exploration into the unknown.

2004 was an extremely exciting year for Furi Furi. Ryosuke and his team toured Berlin's Pictoplasma Conference, Shanghai's Character Licensing Show, Sydney's DiGiT 04 Kuala Lumpur's Undiscovered Territory and California's Game Hotel, besides arranging for the release of their Mummy the Rabbit limited edition figurines at Paris' Colette shop.

Furi Furi characters are akin to radical figures from past Japanese comics in terms of colours and animated features. The ones that stand out are Girl Power Manifesto, Qupu Qupu & Kepu Kepu, Bash 9, Elvis Presley Aloha, Devil's Sweet Smile and the latest FATBEAR USB flash drives. Apart from that, there are the characters featured in the animated films "Shinobi" and "Seed" on Furi Furi's website.

The team is kept busy all year round with commissioned projects for brands such as Ronald McDonalds, Pepsi, Eden's Crush, Gap Kids, Chikro Circus and Meiji. However, Furi Furi is not all about cartoon madness. The key to the company's success is its strong foundation in creativity and a vast degree of imagination invested into every aspect of design.

artist / Ryosuke Tei

location / Japan

website / www.furifuri.com

00 / FATBEAR Series Memory Stick

01

02

01 / Cioccolata Design
02 / Exhibition Display

Photographer: Alexandre Ermel
Mock up: Inés Zaragoza

MADE FOR THE PEOPLE:
HAVAIANAS
www.havaianas.com

" Colour would be our favourite way to play around basically, because we are a fashion accessory and this is one of the best ways to help our consumers impact each day with a fun new look and feeling! "

– Carla Schmitzberger, Havaianas MD –

The word "Brazil" brings to mind the special bond between a country and its nation, a tie that is expressed passionately in fashion, entertainment, culture and dance. One fashion house that certainly taps into this lively mix is Havaianas. Since 1962, its range of psychedelic flip-flops has earned international recognition as an affordable, comfortable and durable footwear. It all began in 1907 when Alpargatas sandals were manufactured for coffee collectors.

From a relatively simple offering of one style in five colours, Havaianas now offers 70 styles in over 500 colours and prints, with an average of 1000 pairs of Havaianas sandals being sold per day.

According to Managing Director of Havaianas, Carla Schmitzberger, consumer behaviour and values are converging towards a more laidback and simple way of life, opting for more modish while functional products, such as fashionable flip-flops. Certainly, the brand manifests a vibrant spirit based on the joy of life, simplicity, authenticity and feeling good physically and emotionally.

While its flagship product was created in 1962 and named Havaianas in 1965, the new strategy was born in 1994, and the decision to tap into the international market, in 2001.

Bikini-clad models and celebrities sashayed down the runway in a series of Havaianas flip-flops at the Sao Paolo Fashion Week. Countless new, cool Havaianas stores at various localities throughout the world have opened. At the same time, the outfit continues to tie up with several top stores, leading brands, and brilliant designers to develop its positioning.

"We are always listening to our consumers to better understand how to meet their needs," says Carla. Reflecting this approach, the brand's history shows a constant improvement in its collections, which may vary for each country. After all, the brand attempts to be receptive to the cultures of the 80 countries in which Havaianas is available.

Throughout it all, it is ultimately the joyful people who drive Havaianas to achieve better quality sandals. It is this quest for a simpler life, Carla says, and enjoying the present moment which Havanaias symbolises.

artist / Carla Schmitzberger • Havaianas MD

location / São Paulo • Brazil

website / www.havaianas.com

Havaianas Alomoana

The Alamoana line brings the shape of
the TOP model with silk-screening; it
is inspired by men's beachwear, with
more refined prints exploring floral and
tribal themes.
Colors and Sizes :
according to market practices.

Collection 2007

havaianas®
kids Pets

Código: 1187
Cor: azul celeste
Colores: azul cielo
Colors: cyanic
Numeração / Tamaños / **Sizes:** 23/4 - 31/2

Código: 1566
Cor: rosa claro
Colores: rosa claro
Colors: light pink
Numeração / Tamaños / **Sizes:** 23/4 - 31/2

Código: 1994
Cor: lavanda
Colores: azul lavanda
Colors: lavander blue
Numeração / Tamaños / **Sizes:** 23/4 - 31/2

Código: 1065
Cor: verde fluor
Colores: verde fluor
Colors: green fluor
Numeração / Tamaños / **Sizes:** 23/4 - 31/2

Kids Pets

A classic of the children's line, Havaianas Kids Pets have animal cutouts on their straps that kids love. The best part – the animals' eyes move!
Colors and Sizes :
according to market practices.

Baby Estampas

The new Baby Estampas bring the theme of "sea life" to this collection. On the sole, fish, octopus and sea turtles steal the scene. The straps, without cut-outs make it easy to match these sandals to any look.

Colors and Sizes :
according to market practices.

01

02

01 / Kids Pets Series Design
02 / Baby Estampas Series Design

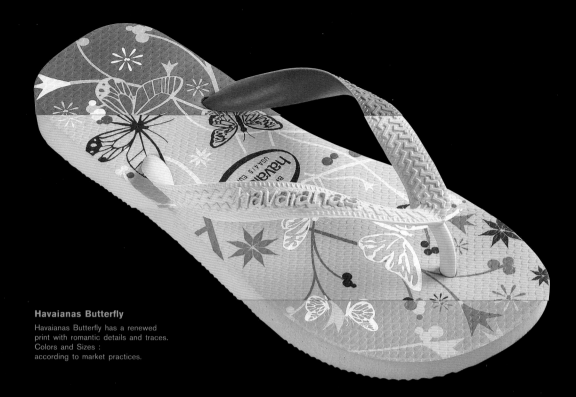

Havaianas Butterfly

Havaianas Butterfly has a renewed
print with romantic details and traces.
Colors and Sizes :
according to market practices.

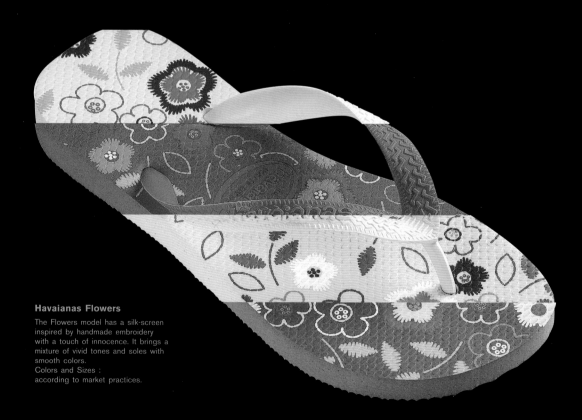

Havaianas Flowers

The Flowers model has a silk-screen
inspired by handmade embroidery
with a touch of innocence. It brings a
mixture of vivid tones and soles with
smooth colors.
Colors and Sizes :
according to market practices.

01

02

01 / Butterfly Series Design
02 / Flower Series Design

artist / Carla Schmitzberger • Havaianas MD

location / São Paulo • Brazil

website / www.havaianas.com

Havaianas Floral

The Floral models takes on new style and personality. Now even more feminine, the sandals have new colors and different combinations of soles and straps.
With a flower and foliage border, this print has been completely redesigned.
Colors and Sizes: according to market practices.
Colors and Sizes :
according to market practices.

havaianas

AS SANDÁLIAS INSPIRADAS
NA LIBERDADE.

POR FAVOR,
GUARDE DO LADO DE FORA
DO ARMÁRIO.

havaianas

EXERÇA
O SEU
DIREITO
DE IR,
ENTRAR,
DANÇAR,
BEBER,
BEIJAR
E VIR.

Havaianas High Butterfly

The new High Butterfly collection
brings you the lightness of butterflies
in harmony with nature, in smooth
color combinations.
Colors and Sizes :
according to market practices.

Havaianas High Cartucho

Bringing in a strong trend, the High
line has yet another new release.
This model combines the attitude of
camouflage with the lightness of roses.
Redesigned shape, profile and strap.
Colors and Sizes: according to market
practices.
Colors and Sizes :
according to market practices.

 01 / Butterfly Series Design
02 / Camuflada Series Design

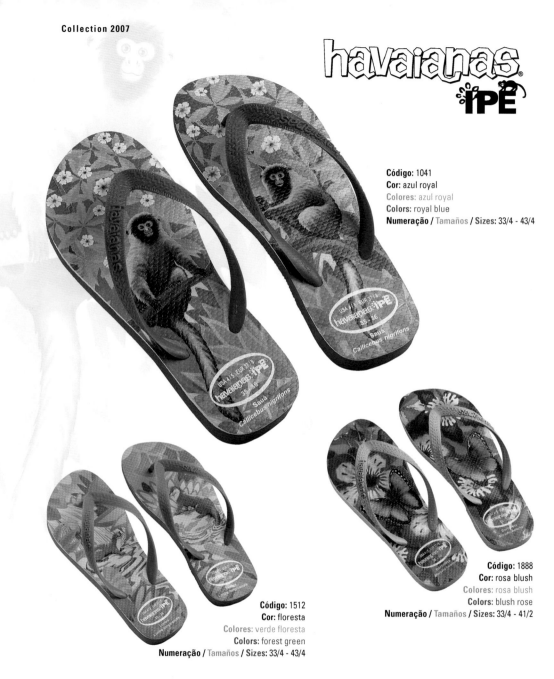

Havaianas IPÊ

Código: 1041
Cor: azul royal
Colores: azul royal
Colors: royal blue
Numeração / Tamaños / **Sizes:** 33/4 - 43/4

Código: 1888
Cor: rosa blush
Colores: rosa blush
Colors: blush rose
Numeração / Tamaños / **Sizes:** 33/4 - 41/2

Código: 1512
Cor: floresta
Colores: verde floresta
Colors: forest green
Numeração / Tamaños / **Sizes:** 33/4 - 43/4

Havaianas Ipê - Ref.: 172000

Para tamanhos maiores do que os mostrados nesta lamina, existe um mínimo de 72 pares/tamanho/cor.
For sizes higher than shown, there is a minimun of 72 pairs/special size/color.
Para numeraciones más grandes de las mostradas en esta hoja, hay un mínimo de 72 pares/talla especial/color.

• Brazilian Sizes. For other countries, please see the conversion list in this catalog. Tamaños Brasileños.
Para otros países, mire en la tabla de conversión en este catálogo. **Tamanhos Brasileiros. Para outros países, procure na tabela de conversão.**

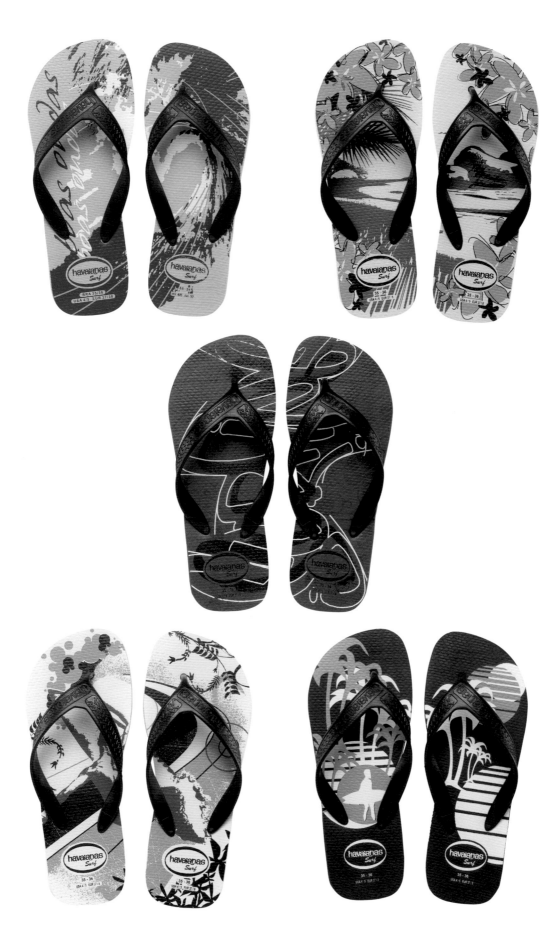

artist / Carla Schmitzberger • Havaianas MD

location / São Paulo • Brazil

website / www.havaianas.com

Havaianas Surf

Surf fashion transcends sport and is a point of reference for style. It is appreciated and used by men of all walks of life. The new prints with drawings maneuvers, landscapes and graphics that reflect the surfer spirit (an outdoor lifestyle in touch with nature). The sandal in more "robust" and masculine, and is extremely comfortable with a wider shape and straps.

Highlight :
Exclusive hanger with surfboard scraper.
Colors and Sizes :
According to market practices.

> " We love blending the classic era with modern spaces and feelings. If you see the Classic Hint Mints in a Cary Grant movie, it would fit. Conversely, if you saw (James) Bond casually pulling a Hint Mint tin from his chest pocket in Casino Royale, it would resonate. "

– Cooper Bates, Vice President of Hint Mint –

When Harley Cross and Cooper Bates were first conceptualised Hint Mint, they wanted to introduce design to a market that, up until 1997, had been devoid of any real creative ingenuity. They didn't have the substantial funding needed for marketing during the first few years of the company's inception in 1988 but Cooper knew that if they could make a beautiful product, people would respond to it.

Take other examples of high design, Cooper suggests, from the technology-driven BMW 7 series that runs on liquid hydrogen or gasoline, to slick PDAs and the innovative iPod through all its incarnations. Design is becoming more and more emotional for people of today's generation, he asserts.

Even just a name is a hook, thought Harley who was very eager to trademark the name "Hint Mint" in 1988. In order to do so however, he had to manufacture the mints beforehand. He spoke to Cooper, his trusted friend, about his inclination and thus a partnership was born. It meant leaving their acting careers aside until Hint Mint was stable enough. In 2000, give or take a few months, Hint Mint was officially born in Los Angeles.

"We obviously can't live inside our designs, but in a sense we are living inside them. I like to wonder – wonder why we don't find community more valuable. If we invested more in community, we would feel more. If we felt more, we would find all the pain and suffering in the world intolerable. I suppose this is all rooted in my upbringing," says Cooper. Indeed, he proposes that there is much power in community, that when there is organization, people can change the course of their lives for the greater good of all.

Doing exactly what he preaches, Hint Mint conducts an Awareness Series for both breast cancer and AIDS where 100% of profits go to charity, as does the Limited Edition Artist Series.

"I think that over the course of the next five years, we are going to see designs on both large and small scale that will blow us all away," says Cooper. "We create designs that people can carry around with them to all parts of the world. Hint Mint is that emotional item."

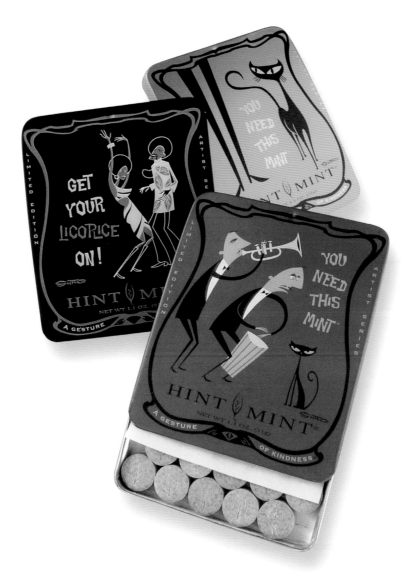

concept design by / Ilaria Marelli • www.ilariamarelli.com
images and info by / sabine.schweigert • www.fastwebnet.it

HIGHLIGHT:
ILARIA
MARELLI
www.ilariamarelli.com

66

The present time offers an exceptional laboratory of cultural and social mixing, local and global sharing of influences as well as technological evolution.

99

– Ilaria Marelli –

Italy's architecture industry needs people like Ilaria Marelli, whose work offers a new way of looking at ordinary things, while considering what's good for Mother Nature. The low-profile architect and designer is also a professor, consultant and founder of her own creative lab, ILARIA MARELLI Studio.

"I really like materials that are ephemeral, for example, paper for origami and kirigami, fabric for kites and wire net. For "solidity", I often use plexiglas, mirror, shiny metal and lacquered white that look immaterial in some way," says Ilaria.

Ilaria was collaborating with contemporary furniture maker Capellini International for five years before she decided to establish her own creative lab in 2003. Things kicked off to a good start when Ilaria won the "Lights of the Future 2004" award, for her energy-efficient Ara floor and wall lamp which take the form of a vertical cut of light. She is also occupied with designing for exhibitions and interiors, as well as in providing product and communication consultancy to design-orientated companies.

Her clients are as diverse as Capellini, Nemo-Cassina, Coin, Variazioni, Pitti Immagine, Invicta, Zanotta, Modal, Aquagirl, Lancia, Franco Maria Ricci, Odry, and Como in Style. In print, her works have graced the pages of glossy magazines such as Wallpaper, Elle Décor, Surface, Details, ADM, Casa International China and Interni.

Besides teaching at the Milan Politecnico in Service and Strategic Design, Ilaria is also one of the main promoters of the first co-housing project in Italy (together with Ezio Manzini and Luca Mortara) which posits a community composed of private homes sharing extensive common facilities.

è una lenta, dolce danza di foglie bianche che oscillano nell'aria
It's a slow and sweet dance of white leaf swinging in the air

New View

poteva fare una lepre turchina? ... "Ce
bambino tornò allora al tavolo e fece l...
la fece diventare un cespuglio.
a neppure il cespuglio gli piaceva e cos...
oi, ecco apparire una nube, ma così gran

The ki...
then ...
Howe...
Then a cloud popped up a...

concept design by / Ilaria Marelli • www.ilariamarelli.com
images and info by / sabine.schweigert • www.fastwebnet.it

artist / Jois Tai / Rex Advincula

location / Manila

website / www.inksurge.com

COFFEE THE BEST TONIC:
INKSURGE
www.inksurge.com

We are doing our best to merge concepts with our visuals. We play a lot with symbols and representations in terms of elements and illustrations.

– Inksurge –

Design studio Inksurge from Manila, the Philippines, finds that their best works come out of late nights blending concepts with innovative visuals and sufficient amounts of coffee, no doubt. After all, founders, Jois Tai and Rex Advincula are fans of a good brew. The former likes it with milk while the latter takes it with sugar, which almost describes the fusion of different talents that makes up Inksurge's eclectic design skills.

In December 2001, Jois and Rex decided that they wanted something different from their monotonous routine at the IT firm where they were working. In a pitch of enterprise, Inksurge was formed in 2002.

There were times when they just wanted to sit back, relax and enjoy long sips of the strong black stuff as they watched the world go round. Nevertheless inspiration was not lacking and their late nights paid off as clients such as MTV Singapore, MTV Philippines, Animax, EMI Philippines and

several others in the entertainment industry began recognising their art.

Besides speaking at the conferences OFFF '04 (Spain) and Graphika Manila (Philippines), Inksurge have submitted illustrations and logo designs to DPI Magazine, Computer Arts, Tres Logos, Play Loud! and books such as Jeremyville, People Like Us Collections and Hooked Clothings.

Inksurge have also explored other graphic design-based disciplines, including fashion design and album cover design, for which they won the Awit Award for best album packaging in 2007 for their work for Filipino band, SugarFree.

If it's true that designers tend to live inside their works, Jois and Rex are no exceptions. They like infusing elements that tickle their own funny bones but only after they work around the concepts seriously.

artist Jois Tai / Rex Advincula

location / Manila

website / www.inksurge.com

Inksurge Table Lamp

description /
Design printed inverse. Design only
appears when light is on.

Puzzle Table

description /
In collaboration with furniture designer
Doy Lagos. This 0.35 meters x 0.40
meters per piece puzzle table combines to a big one. Design was laser-
etched on Narra with a varnish finish.

Wall Tiles

description /
8" x 8" wall tiles, design digitally
printed on ceramic

artist / Jois Tai / Rex Advincula

location / Manila

website / www.inksurge.com

artist / Jon Burgerman

location / Nottingham • UK

website / www.jonburgerman.com / www.biro-web.com

THE DOODLE EXPERT:

JON
BURGERMAN

www.jonburgerman.com

" Of course, I like to dabble with other materials including paints, marker pens, different paper stocks and the computer but drawing with a pen on a clean piece of paper is what I like to do best. "

– Jon Burgerman –

As long as Jon Burgerman can remember, he went to infants' school wearing a little cap and enjoyed playing in the sand pit. He enjoyed football too, and watched cartoons and films he borrowed from his dad's video shop. Sometimes he would dance in private to the music of Michael Jackson played on his walkman. He could have been a great dancer if he had practised as much as he did with his art.

His art, however, he did develop, having studied that for his A-Levels and then advanced to Fine Art at Nottingham Trent University. This is where he began being bombarded with opportunities to feed his artistic appetite.

No less than anywhere else, Jon was out and about in the streets where trends and people collided. His senses were quick to respond to new rave graphics; bright, bold, handmade but slick illustrations and designs veering off the pages and screens into many fantastical new forms.

The results of which, and for which he's most well known, is his doodling -- wonky, happy, dumb and wrong as he describes it. "It's a muddled up, scribbly sort of place

as everything merges into one, overlaps and gets in the way of my drawings."

He also owes his success to a delicate 20-80 mix of hard work and good luck. Growing up in the middle of UK during the 1980's and 90's taught him to react to things with wide eyes and low expectations. Ever since he became a designer and illustrator, lots of things and people have inspired him.

In fact, Jon's art has secured spots in various publications, such as Latex for Fun, the Jeremyville Sessions book published by idN, If You Could Do Anything Tommorow, Los Logos 3, Pictoplasma 'The Character Encyclopaedia' – The great new book from Pictoplasma, 300% Cotton, Tattoo Icons, The Art of Rebellion 2, and Print and Production for Promotional Items.

Doodling on cardboards, paper, walls and objects for a living, sometimes, he gets sucked in to his work until late at night, not socialising at all. He reckons that it's good not to think about design, illustrations, doodles and art all the time however, just for peace of mind. These, then, would be good times to put on the old Michael Jackson again.

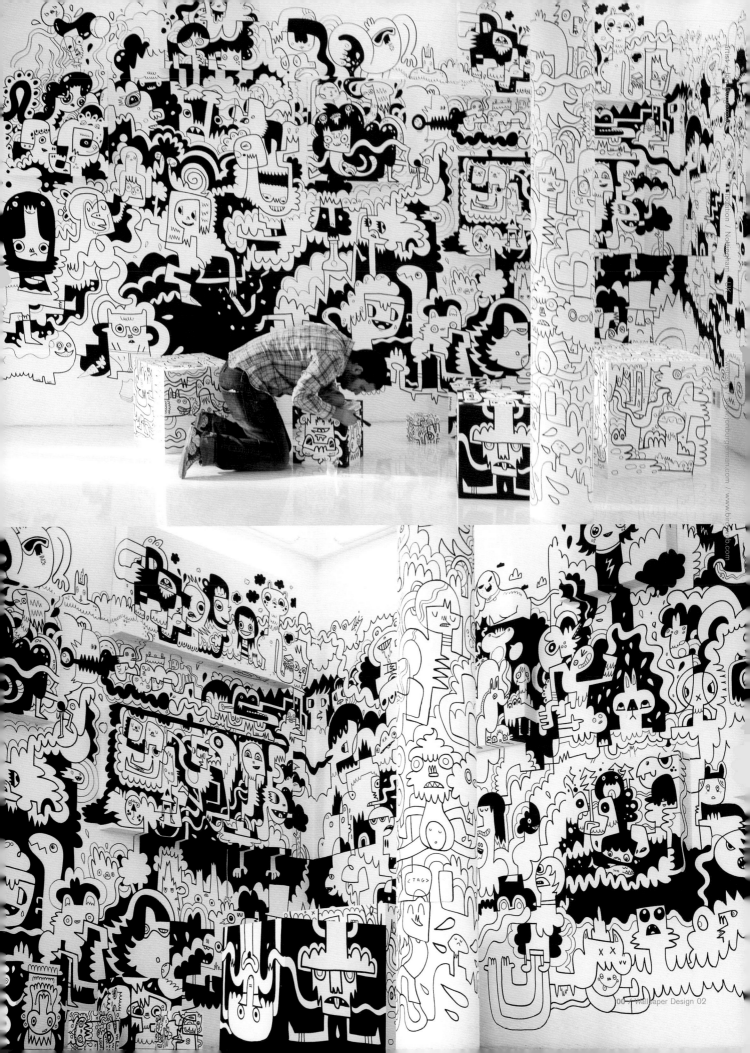

Hotel 60, Riccione, Italy
June 2006

01
02

01 / Wallpaper Design 03
02 / Tent Design

01 / Stationery Set Design
02 / Cushion Design
03 / Box Design
04 / Belt Design

artist / Jurgen Bey

location / The Netherlands

website / www.jurgenbey.nl

F1.08

photography by / Roel van Tour

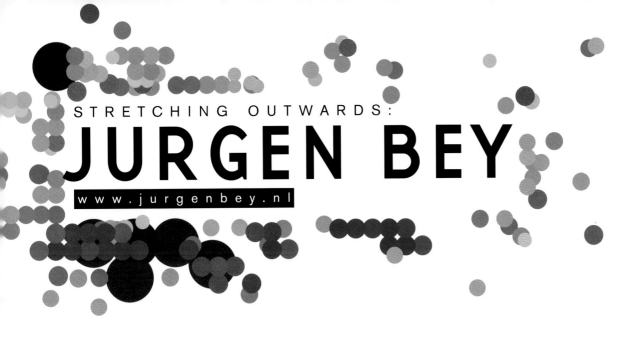

STRETCHING OUTWARDS:
JURGEN BEY

www.jurgenbey.nl

> " I will never retire from designing. Maybe I would because design is not forever. I've tried an amount of things at different levels and speeds. That's why I teach a lot now. "

– Jurgen Bey –

Jurgen Bey from the Netherlands, who would prefer to be called a product designer rather than an interior designer, finds inspiration in day-to-day life, believing that looking at people and objects on our planet can trigger not one but many ideas. He is the sort of man who thinks spontaneously and not infrequently envisions the future.

Jurgen Bey wanted to become a veterinarian when he was a kid. Instead, when interning in Barcelona, he fell in love with industrial design. Now, he follows a round-the-clock working schedule at his studio in Rotterdam.

The former student of Design Academy Eindhoven has for example, put some thought into reinventing old, boring furniture. Using a stretchable fibre made of PVC that was widely used in the history of aviation and locomotives during the Second World War, he decorates old furniture to produce an interesting skin-like outer layer.

On an ordinary day, 42-year-old Jurgen's favourite activities involve a series of physi-

cal observations of people and objects. Blessed with an eye for detail and a conceptual mind, his products are designed to speak the language of reality. Nothing can beat the world as the biggest supplier of ideas; and armed with that knowledge, Jurgen has realised a kaleidoscope of brilliant works made out of several materials.

Nature is priceless and Jurgen believes that if we were able to understand this we could be living in a new world. After all, he desires to create a new skin for everybody to live in and grow as a whole. By placing nature at a good position throughout execution, his products are earth-friendly, stylish and spacious.

As you can see, it is Jurgen's curiosity and eagerness to change the ways people run their lives that continues spurring him on in this lifetime career of industrial design. A firm believer in the theory of evolution, Jurgen feels a need to continuously travel and open up to new cultures in the hopes that he can in his own way find effective solutions to the bigger problems of the universe.

artist / Jurgen Bey

location / The Netherlands

website / www.jurgenbey.nl

stuffz ▼ 202 • 203 ▲

photography by / Roel van Tour

00 / HTR Interior Design

artist / Jurgen Bey

location / The Netherlands

website / www.jurgenbey.nl

photography by / Roel van Tour

Ear-chair has got ears to create privacy or define space
and an arm-rest which forms a small table.
Originally Ear-chair was developed for the reception-room
of Interpolis, an indemnity insurance company.   There are
three different lengths of ears to make different combinations with a various amount of chairs.
The ear-chairs form (with at least a couple) the room.
The outside of the chair is always grey, the inside can
be changed per 'room' so that every room gets its own
character.

Studio Makkink & Bey / Collection PROOFF - SV / 2002

Ear-chair has got ears to create privacy or define space and an arm-rest which forms a small table.

Originally Ear-chair was developed for the reception-room of Interpolis, an indemnity insurance company. There are three different lengths of ears to make different combinations with a various amount of chairs.

The ear-chairs form (with at least a couple) the room. The outside of the chair is always grey, the inside can be changed per 'room' so that every room gets its own character.

design by / Studio Makkink & Bey for Interpolis
assisted by / Silvijn van der Velden / Christiaan Oppewal / Toya Verberne / 2002

Day-tripper is a seven meter long city-bench for Tokyo, Japan.
Day-tripper is based on a study of the different postures people assume on the street during a day, while learning, sitting, lounging, or squatting. Seven of these postures have been fixed and have shaped the wave-like form of this work. More formal pieces of "furniture" have been integrated in this wave – like a dining table, a coffee table or chairs. Working initially from an appreciation of European scale and culture, in this case the designers have chosen to fabricate the works using a skin of fiberglass, printed with a white flower decoration over pink colored polyester.

Studio Makkink & Bey / for Droogdesign
assisted by / Silvijn v/d Velden, Christiaan Oppewal
/ 2002

artist / Francois Verdet / Christelle Chambre

location / Lyon • France

website / www.kanardo.com

CURIOSITY FOR DESIGN:
KANARDO
www.kanardo.com

> " Analogue and digital cameras, bikes and decals... After having our own premises, we now work from home with 3 Macs and a decent Internet connection. "
>
> – Kanardo –

Former journalist Francois Verdet and photojournalist Christelle Chambre set up Kanardo in the heart of Lyon, France in 1999.

"To be honest, Kanardo was first of all the fruit of a love story before it became a professional collaboration. We have, as you may gather, many things in common...," says Verdet. One of the most important things is the principle of allowing creativity free reign.

Living in the 90's was very interesting for the duo. Before the age of wireless networking, people had exclusivity to grand exhibitions and special screenings. Today, the World Wide Web has changed everything – from the way news is digitally disseminated to the public to the birth of an electronic community.

"Each project/product has its website and millions of blogs that review the latest trends," he adds.

Looks like another thing has changed: graphic designers are now playing in the three-dimensional real worlds, terrorising objects and concrete platforms with illustrations.

"A few years ago, we were working for printed paper documents. Today, we've done many designs like decorating cars and vespas. That's funny to play with 3D moving surfaces!"

Kanardo's latest portfolio includes works commissioned by Computer Arts magazine, Xplicid t-shirt club, Pimp my Scoota Vespa decals, Trexi Custom toys and Premiere Vision Fabric Show. Also, they have exhibited at the Pop'n Flop'n group exhibition about sweets (also featuring Genevieve Gauckler and 123Klan) and the Love Original Project vinyl toys show in Tokyo, both in 2006.

"It's our shared view of the world. It's the label (Kanardo) behind which we prefer to withdraw for it is more representative of our works – commercial or artistic – than our names that drift in isolation," Verdet explains. "We use it as a brand to labelise or to produce limited series of products."

On the face of it, Kanardo seems to stand out from the design community in France. One part of it must be the flexibility they have with the things they do, which allows them more breathing space, and also grounds on which to test their ideas.

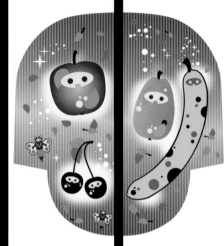

Kanardo™
Anna + The Magic Seeds™

artist / Francois Verdet / Christelle Chambre

location / Lyon • France

website / www.kanardo.com

Cars are the biggest products we have been working for. In fact we don't sell the cars but some adhesive sets to decore vehicles!

Customized 10 and 3 inches Trexi
(Play Imaginative) used for several
exhibitions in France.

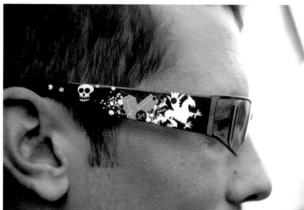

Ty Von Dickxit "Wichawiche live mix"
CD+DVD package

01 / Trexi Custom Design
02 / Glasses Design
03 / T-shirt Design
04 / CD+DVD packaging Design

Illustrations printed on "French espadrilles"
for The String Republic - Exhibition at Artazart / Paris

00 / ACME Symbol Pen Design

VISIONARY:
KARIM RASHID
www.karimrashid.com

> " I am not a brand – I am a designer. But the world understands brands, so I turn to being understood, to being seen, as a brand. "
>
> – Karim Rashid –

Born in Cairo in 1960 and raised in Canada, Karim Rashid is a man of his word and very much into technology and the possibilities of the future. He is currently working, for example, with a fast food restaurant to design bio-degradable packaging using starch and potatoes that has the exact appearance of plastic and that is actually injection-moulded.

"I would argue that plastic is now part of our nature. This is the inevitable course of our existence," Karim explains.

Indeed, one would think of style as a universal statement that dictates our behaviour and delineates what is acceptable. Take for example the present rococo revival – baroque chandeliers, flower motifs and ornate ornamentation. Karim feels otherwise however.

"We are alive today so we should be surrounding ourselves with physical goods that are a reflection of our milieu instead of borrowing derivatives from the past to reinvent something new" he says.

In fact, Karim believes that it is important to not over-embellish a product or space, and to keep a certain truth to it – one that is human and that would touch the sensual side of people.

A designer is a humaniser of manufacture. A designer is also the soul giver to banal objects and spaces and shapes the contemporary world. Thus, the kinds of shapes and forms that will load the spaces of tomorrow will have their own set of semantic language, enhanced functions, better textures and greater ability to speak to humans, according to Karim.

"Love and desire are part of my interests in 'sensualising' our physical, material world. I do this, not just through design development, but by lecturing about technology, about human behaviour, about social, political and artistic agendas. I feel I must inspire. That's my goal."

No one sees it like Karim does. He who travels 180 days a year measures ev-

ery detail of life – of the universal yet shrinking world and the accelerating burst of technology – as inspiring. This practitioner has experienced different design movements that orbit around him, as well as some inspiring and tainted moments.

This creative wants to be the motivator to empower the individual, while helping shape the physical world, infusing positive thinking and healthy living into people's lives through design and lectures.

If he weren't famous for his philosophies and designs, he wouldn't have his name imprinted or even given mention in hundreds of books and magazines, publication after publication, year after year. But he is. Both in quality and in physique, from his remarkable contributions to design to being above 6 feet tall with a killer fashion sense, Karim Rashid is too big a figure to overlook.

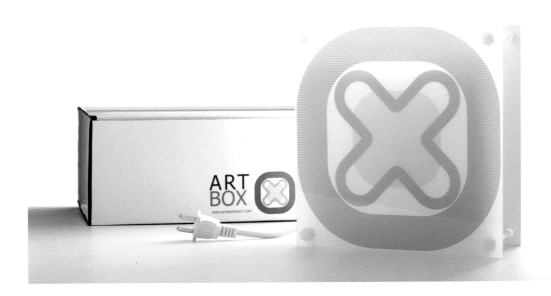

01 / ACME Megan Bag Design
02 / Art Box Design

00 / Aitali Series Design

01 / Sofa Chairs Design
02 / Aitali Tables Design

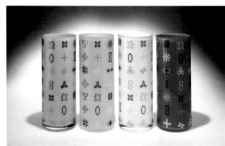

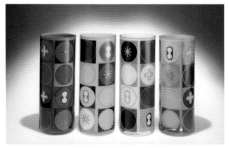

01 / Entrex Series Cups Design
02 / MENU Thermo Cups Design
03 / Egizia Series Design

01 02

01 / Entrex Series Design
02 / Entrex Series Design

01
02

01 / Bitossi Series Design
02 / AUDI Car Skin Design

Karim Rashid Loft

designer / Karim Rashid
design team / Dennis Askins / Camila Tariki
client / Karim Rashid
location / New York, NY
photos by / Jean Francois Jussaud
furniture & fixtures / vendors

furniture and lighting designed by /
Karim for Frighetto / Curvet / Umbra /
Magis / Nienkamper / Zeritalia / Foscarini
/ MGlass / Fasem / Kovacs / Foscarini
/ Idee / Edra / Galerkin / Offect / Pure
Design / Softgoods / Label

artist / Katrin Olina

location / Hong Kong

website / www.katrin-olina.com

SKIN - Aesthetic Medical Clinic • Florence • Italy
interior Design / Michael Young
graphic art work / Katrin Olina
photography / Carlo Lavatori
project architect and management / Alberto Puchetti & Paolo Romagnoli
furniture / Cap Spa / Magis / MK Maeda Japan / Innermost / Cesarre Terraneo
floor surfaces / Dupont SGX Laminate / Dupont Corian
wall Surfaces / Dupont SGX Laminate / Dupont Corian
client / Kalloni srl

KATRINOLINA LTD:
KATRIN-OLINA
www.katrin-olina.com

" I play around with stuff, and stuff can be as immaterial as it can be material. "

– Katrin Olina Petursdottir –

Switzerland's Montreux Jazz Festival has long cultivated a collaborative relationship with designers and artists. One of these is Iceland-based Katrin Olina Petursdottir who in 2007 became the second woman to design the festival's prestigious poster after Niki de Saint Phalle in 1984.

Since graduating in product design at Paris' E.S.D.I. (School of Industrial Design), she's been building up a different kind of graphic language. The results are works which are diverse and applicable to anything from products, fashion, textiles to interiors.

"Every project I do is an expedition, or at least a field trip into my subconscious mind. My working method is instinctive as I'm more interested in the subjective than the objective at the end of the day. I draw my illustrations with a computer and it feels just as close to making music or even writ-

ing. When I'm working on a piece, I will totally immerse myself into it. For me, it's more about the journey than the destination," Petursdottir explains.

She worked for Philippe Stark in Paris and Ross Lovegrove in London from 1996 to 1997, before partnering with her husband, Michael Young, at his studio in Reykjavik. Iceland is far less stressful but nonetheless wild and subdued. It's a place that calls for introspection and definitely fertilises the imagination.

In 2005 meanwhile, Petursdottir was commissioned by the National Gallery in Oslo to create a 10 meter by 5 meter masterpiece for the international art show Kiss the Frog – the Art of Transformation. Today, Petursdottir is probably one of Iceland's best exports and like the frog, her destiny has certainly been changing for the better.

SKIN - Aesthetic Medical Clinic • Florence • Italy

SKIN - Aesthetic Medical Clinic • Florence • Italy

interior Design / Michael Young
graphic art work / Katrin Olina
photography / Carlo Lavatori
project architect and management / Alberto Puchetti & Paolo Romagnoli
furniture / Cap Spa / Magis / MK Maeda Japan / Innermost / Cesarre Terraneo
floor surfaces / Dupont SGX Laminate / Dupont Corian
wall Surfaces / Dupont SGX Laminate / Dupont Corian
client / Kalloni srl

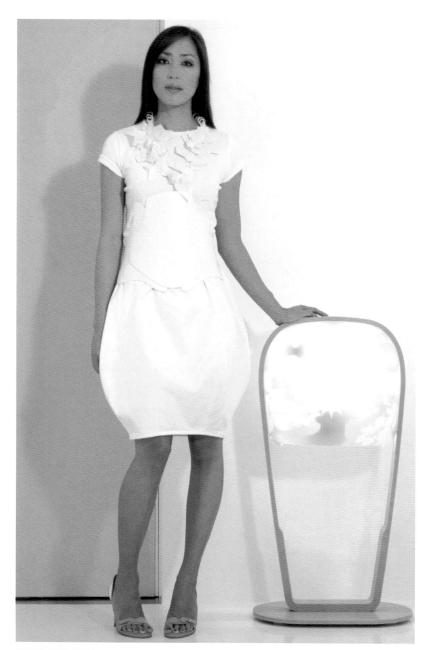

SKIN - Uniform Design

graphic art work / Katrin Olina

photography / Carlo Lavatori

00 / Skin Uniform Design

A collection of limited edition products, produced by Katrin Olina ltd.

100% silk scarf, with art work featuring a crime riddle by Katrin Olina

A collection of limited edition products, produced by Katrin Olina ltd.

Porcelain dishes painted by hand, featuring Noc, the grinning ghost and Trumpet head by Katrin Olina

Snowboards & Helmets

Limited edition by Katrin Olina ltd.
At Gallery i8, Reykjavik, Iceland 2006
date of production • 2006

designer / Katrin Olina (Petursdottir)
illustrator / Katrin Olina (Petursdottir)

00 / K-Hooland Series Design

EVERY PART A DAYDREAMER:
KUANTH
www.kuanth.com

" I use fabric, acrylic, paper and wood. Canvas has always been my favourite material simply because it's blank. I'm sure there're more interesting materials yet to be discovered. "

– Kuanth –

After five years of working in the publishing industry, and equipped with a year of experience in advertising, Malaysian Kuanth turned freelance illustrator in 2002. For someone who has never dreamt this big, the Singapore-based designer has worked with big industrial players such as Nokia, Panasonic, Pepsi, CK Tangs, Bata, Nescafe, SIA, Lancome, Sony and Heineken.

Kuanth certainly knows what makes a good designer. "I think we are moving towards simplicity and functionality but also being expressive with our thoughts and personalities at the same time," says the graduate from The One Academy in Kuala Lumpur, Malaysia.

It's definitely tough for Kuanth at first but he asserts that as people learn more from mistakes, the better they become at what they do. "That's why I have created a brand of my own – Mistake by Kuanth – to do what I love to do." he adds. Lest that he has no desire to cross bridges and experiment on new things.

An exclusive interview with Singapore's leading design magazine iSh revealed a younger version of Kuanth when he was still an aspiring designer. During that time, he already mustered 50% desire on doodles and doll-making. The remaining ingredient was found in his impalpable style. Take the Oh L'Amour Nokia ad campaign

for example, such brilliant effects would not have been achievable if not for his hard work and fervour for beautiful things.

He is every part like a daydreamer. He sort of had a bout of depressions when he was a teen. "I was suicidal back then simply because I had to do the housework and my brother didn't have to," he says, "but as I looked out from the balcony which was two floors up, the concrete ground seemed tougher than doing the housework. It didn't take long to get myself back into the house and finish my chores." That goes to say something about the way he works.

True enough, says Kuanth who has done editorial illustrations for Amoeba, Cleo, Seventeen, Torque, Her World, Vmag and Nu You, "Everything to me is like a blank piece of canvas. I conceptualise and execute what I have in mind onto any subject or object that inspires me no matter the medium or material."

During Tiger Translate 2007 in New York organised by Tiger Beer, Kuanth added a personal touch to the site installation featuring live drawings of faces and words on 35 boxes. Others who participated in the international showcase were design collective Surface to Air, Malaysian mix-media designer Stephen Lau and Singaporean photographer Jing.

artist / Kuanth

location / Singapore

website / www.kuanth.com / www.kuanth.blogspot.com

00 / K-Hooland Series Design

00 / Maxalot Outdoor Display

IMAGINARY SEQUENCE:
KUSTAA SAKSI

www.kustaasaksi.com

> " Kustaa Saksi's drawings have even taken the form of cool building-sized mural prints at multiple locations around the heart of New York. "

He got the whole world in his hands. Design enthusiasts would probably agree with the statement, and that Kustaa Saksi is one of the few illustrators who can find order in the chaotic world of graphic design. His illustrations are often acknowledged as part of an essential "lexicon of illustration" because of his exquisite colour palettes.

In recent years, Finnish Kustaa took with him his prized talent on a plane to Paris for a long-term career there. Kustaa then started attracting many eyes to his intuitive style there. Indeed, he has garnered several gigs illustrating for fashion brands such as Lacoste, Issey Miyake, Diesel, Levi's, as well as magazines such as Arkitip, Playboy, Sleazenation, Elle and Wallpaper.

His drawings have even taken the form of cool building-sized mural prints at multiple locations around the heart of New York City, as commissioned by Brazilian flip flops maker, Havaianas. Recently, Kustaa also spoke at the Massive Territory Design Conference and Mines International Design Intelligence (MIDI) Convention in Kuala Lumpur, Malaysia.

Each of his project is designed in the truest Finnish way – to retain that appreciation for psychedelia and combine it with a flawless, shiny effect – and yet results in a style that is wholly Kustaa Saksi.

00 / Maxalot Outdoor Display

artist / Kustaa Saksi

location / Finland

website / www.kustaasaksi.com

01
02

01 / Shoes Design
02 / Clothes Design

FASHION FAST FORWARD:

L&A MAETHGER

www.l-a-maethger.com

66 In fashion design, there are the classifieds and categories – high fashion, street wear, casual, etc. We try to mix it up, to create our own style that is free of any border or limit. So many fashion labels are trying to make only nice clothes but they are lacking a strong statement. Our collection tells you a story of our life and this we want to share with the people wearing it. 99

– L&A Maethger –

Hailing from Germany, twin brothers Lucas and Aaron Maethger reinforced Brussels' reputation as a fashion hotspot when in 2005 they presented their first collection of mesh that was deemed as completely bold and modish by people in the country. Lucas graduated in fashion design from Antwerp's Academy of Fine Arts in 2003 with an already outstanding portfolio of fashion-related activities and exhibitions, when Aaron joined him, thus sparking off another classic tale of "the brothers gonna work it out".

It all began, you could say, when on the lookout for opportunities in 2003, Aaron moved to Belgium to be with his brother. It was after he helped out with Lucas' assignment that Aaron decided to stay and indulge in their common love for fashion. The freedom to invent was so seductive that the enterprising duo made it a quest to find a niche in this challenging field.

The two followed on their successful debut with collections based on the themes URBAN (SS07) and HEROES (AW2007/08). Here, L&A Maethger adopted the textures of wooden floor patterns, glass building blocks, apartment blocks and some of the world's great architecture as overprints. Inspiration was constantly also refreshed by intensely searching for contacts with all kinds of artists with whom to exchange ideas and views, and being open about it. The result is clothes that are bold and sophisticated while still being wearable and comfortable, boasting of finer details when it comes to stitches and motifs.

More of the urban environment looks set to become the brothers' playground as their future fast forwards beyond Brussels, armed with great collections that tell a story.

location / Taiwan

website / www.match-b.com

MODERN FIRE LIGHTER:

MATCH-BOND

www.match-b.com

❝ We're good at printing products using the right choice of paper. In the future, we'll try out other kinds of raw materials based on the product we design. It can be metal, fabric or even food-related material. ❞

– Match-Bond –

Cavemen were able to light a fire with stones and twigs which marked the beginning of an era of civilisation. Since then, ignition has been achieved courtesy of the matchbox and then, the lighter. These days however, there has been a revival of interest in matchboxes, and no least by Taiwan-based Match-Bond.

The Match-Bond crew have reason to believe that this conventional medium will return to popular demand because they believe that there are tons of irreplaceable emotions within a matchbox. They reckon that it has the power to convey a message to the world effectively and has a part in keeping the spirit of rock n' roll alive.

Match-Bond was founded in 2005 by 25in design group, a design company which also handles other visual works for

big companies such as SONY Computer Entertainment International and rock music festivals. By 2006, the idea of Match-Bond matchboxes took off at the Rock n' Roll Music Festival in Taiwan.

Check out the Wildlife Conservation Series, which consists of four matchboxes designed with scary monsters with pointed names such as SOS Polar Bear, Brokeback Shark, Husky and Eunuch Tiger. The opening of the box reveals a big mouth of the monster which tells people that monsters are loud when need be.

"In order to convey the idea of protecting wildlife, we wanted to make it less boring and serious so we designed several pitiful little animals with a sense of humour attached to each of the four."

Brokeback Shark

Human cut its fins as ambrosia food , so it fixs the surfboard fin on its back with painful and anger.

Eunuch Tiger

Not correct knowing , make the tigers killed at random , so we use the Chinese traditional eunuch images to let people notice this problem by humor way.

Husky

When pet becomes popular , forsake will be the serious problem , husky was from the north pole ,without the correct raised , the tropical weather will make it hard to live.

SOS Polar Bear

It loses its habitat and depends the swim tube to float on the sea . and hides the

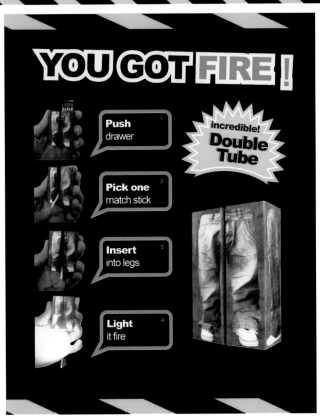

location / The Netherlands

website / www.marcelwanders.com

photography by / Alberto Ferrero / 2005
contact photographer before using images
mail@albertoferrero.it

LOVE, LIVE AND DREAM:
MARCEL WANDERS
www.marcelwanders.com

❝ I have never made babies with a PUMA, but now they have been born, it is hard to say whose genetics are most obvious. ❞

– Marcel Wanders –

Marcel Wanders' iconic Knotted Chair, which he produced for Droog Design in 1996, slid open the door of fame for him. Indeed, it's interesting to peek into the life of the man, synonymous with Marcel Wanders Studio (MWS), who became the epitome of contemporary Dutch design.

Having grown up in Boxtel in the Netherlands and now in his early 40s, Wanders has stamped on the grounds all over Europe for exhibitions, art installations, press conferences, projects, collaborations, contracts and interviews with publication houses. Those that have interviewed him, namely I.D Magazine, Wallpaper, Elle Decoration, Icon, Esquire, The International Herald Tribune, Washington Post, the Financial Times, the New York Times and Business Week, are likely to say that this enterprising man really does wonders with design.

Wanders himself heads the MWS studio in Amsterdam and behind all that business dealings, he lives up to a great motto: "Here to create an environment of love, Live with passion and Make our most exciting dreams come true."

In 2000, he started working on Moooi, overseeing the project's art direction and corporate identity and running its new line of high-end, sophisticated furniture.

Not surprisingly, several awards have followed. In 2005, MWS was dubbed by The Observer as one of the most inspiring powerhouses of multi-disciplinary design. In 2006 meanwhile, he was awarded 'Designer of the Year' at the Elle Decoration International Design Awards.

In fact, Wanders' magic wand doesn't just touch the likes of sofas and furniture. At Design Boston 2006, he announced that he was creating design-focused accessories for Puma's Spring 2007 collection.

With some special wallpaper, he furthermore transformed the already pretty villa PUMA selected for the launch of the collection into an absolute hangout. The concept was to create an urban touch that would stimulate a relaxing mood among the party-goers and socialites while enjoying their cold champagne.

Wanders also plays a stellar role in charity. In 2001, he founded and ran the Can of Gold Project with proceeds going to the homeless and disadvantaged in Hamburg, Sydney and London. He has also contributed to KiKa, an organisation that funds cancer reseach and supports children with cancer, by designing the KiKa Award.

Indeed, he has worked hard to get this far. There is the pressure to perform at work and also to maintain a low-key life but ultimately there is little or none that can poison his passion for the arts.

All mosaic walls are specially designed by / Marcel Wanders studio
produced by / Bisazza
sponsors / Bisazza - Art on Tiles
photography by / George Terberg

photography by / Inga Powilleit
styling by / Tatjana Quax

00 / Lute Suite Design

Mosaic table • "One Morning They Woke Up" by /
Marcel Wanders (Bisazza)
produced by / Bisazza

sponsors / Bisazza - Art on Tiles
photography by / Alberto Ferrero / 2005

wallpaper design by / Marcel Wanders studio
floor & metal tiles by / Marcel Wanders studio
bath tub - soap bath by / Marcel Wanders - Bisazza

wall with printed tiles - design by / Marcel Wanders - Art on Tiles
photography by / Alberto Ferrero / 2005

marcel wanders ® studio

All mosaic walls are specially designed by / Marcel Wanders studio
produced by / Bisazza
sponsors / Bisazza - Art on Tiles
photography by / Alberto Ferrero / 2005

photographer / Inga Powilleit
styling / Tatjana Quax

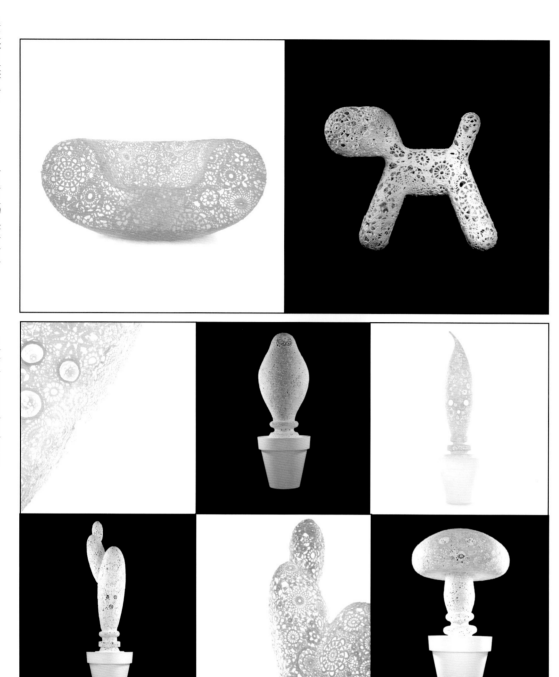

01
02

01 / Topiary Series Design
02 / Plates Design

01

02

01 / Cappellini Series Light Design
02 / Chest of Boxes Design

WANDERS
WONDERS

00 / Marcel Wander for PUMA Series Design

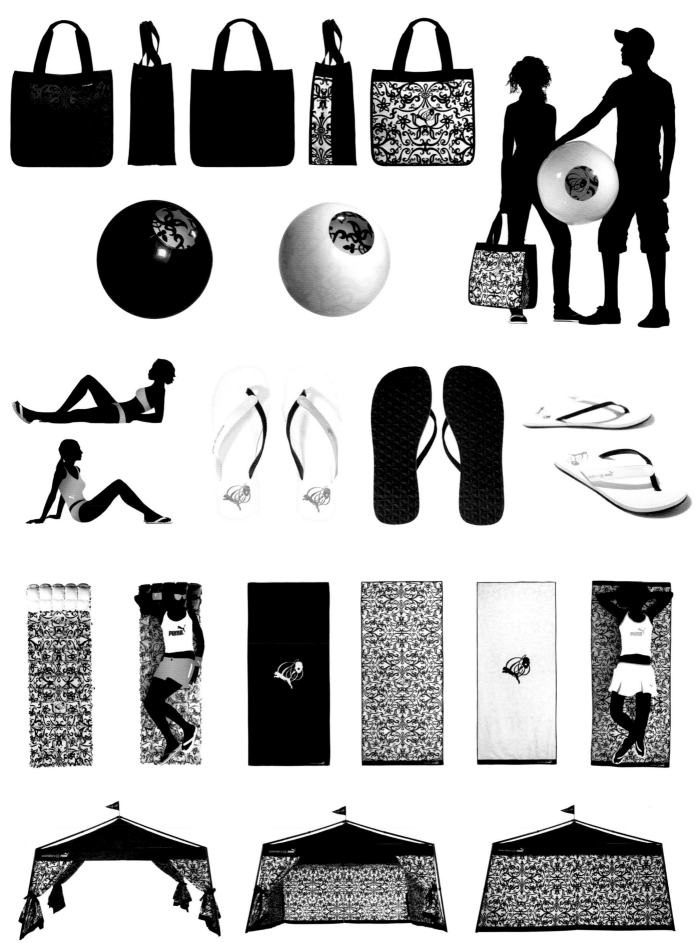

MARKUS BENESCH CREATES

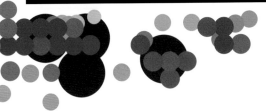

> " Usually I follow a theme which leads me through a project. It could either be a very personal one or one given to me externally by a client. I hardly ever design anything just for fun or without a specific purpose. "
>
> – Markus Benesch –

Markus Benesch was only 18 years old when he coordinated his first interior project for a Benetton store in Munich. He never got accepted into university however. Yet he went back as a visiting professor later in his illustrious career.

Not having a campus life at that time urged young Benesch to continue working as an interior designer, renovator and architect. He probably went through hard times pitching for jobs against big design companies. Nonetheless, he wasn't fazed by constant letdowns. Instead, he foresaw opportunities. At 21 in fact, he was offered work as a furniture designer with Swiss furniture maker, Modular.

"Strangely, today I work with and for people I admired 17 years ago," says Benesch who in 2000 founded his own studio under the name Markus Benesch Creates (MBC). MBC is an industrial and interior design studio with a focus on the wallpaper and laminate industry, as well as designs for a multitude of furniture, lights, materials and spaces. His favourite materials right now are foam, laminates, wallpaper, all kind of fibres and of course the Silversurfer laminate which he invented in 1998 for lightcubes and lamps.

Currently, MBC has mutually beneficial relationships with companies such as Abey Laminati, Benetton, Esselte Leitz, Rasch, Neue Modular and Paul Smith to name a few. His projects such as Money for Milan, Colorface, La Casa Di Alice and others have been published in more than 780 articles and 11 books.

It all boils down to Markus Benesch Creates' aim to serve existing functional needs and to anticipate future desires. Markus also receives inspiration in all forms: in the shape of people, the nature and a muse "who knows how to trigger good stuff out of me" whenever he lacks of inspiration.

artist / Markus Benesch

location / Milano • Italy • Munich • Germany

website / www.markusbenesch.com

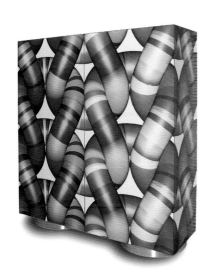

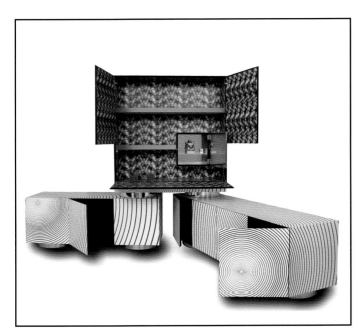

photography by / Andreas Pollok / Benni Konte / Patrik Spaeth

photography by / Andreas Pollok / Benni Konte / Patrik Spaeth

00 / Honey Table Design

photography by / Andreas Pollok / Benni Konte / Patrik Spaeth

photography by / Laura Rizzi

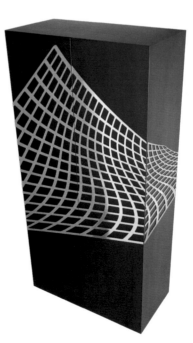

photography by / Laura Rizzi

01

02

01 / Showroom Milano 2004
02 / Furniture Design

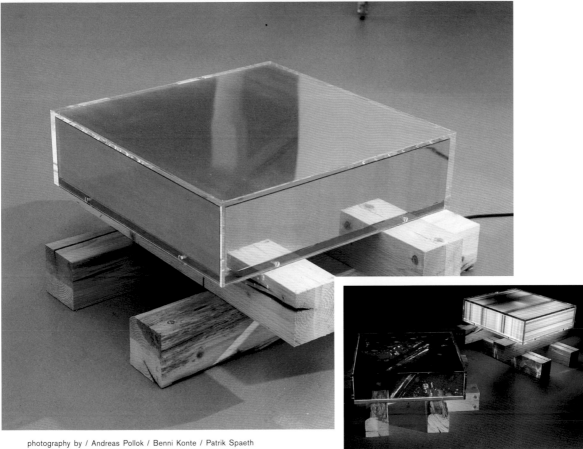

photography by / Andreas Pollok / Benni Konte / Patrik Spaeth

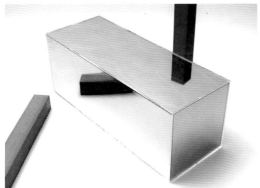

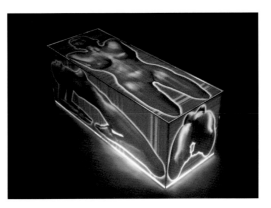

photography by / Andreas Pollok / Benni Konte / Patrik Spaeth

01 / Cube Series Design
02 / Adonia Design

00 / Ginchy Series Design

DESIGNER TOY X NEW TECH MEDIA:
MIMOCO

www.mimoco.com

" The mimobot concept integrates two very different mediums – toys as a canvas and flash memory as a digital distribution vehicle – to result in a new kind of interactivity and experience for end users. "

– mimoco –

Mimobots are more than just functioning USB flash drives – they are also collectibles designed by artists worldwide, a trend that's altering the way that media can communicate. mimobots are entertaining, stylish and data friendly. The man behind mimoco, the studio where mimobots come true, is Evan Blaustein.

Mimoco does not bear any meaning in the Japanese language but it rings just as well as "memory". When its founder Evan Blaustein was still in school, he'd known that USB flash drives could be a designer toy in years to come. His gut feelings assuring him that it would work, he later formed the mimoco team to produce a prototype.

The mimobot shape was created by industrial design lead, Baron Brandt, while the technical features were achieved with the expertise of engineer, Todd Taylor. On the lookout for the right candidate to illustrate meanwhile, Evan stumbled upon some designs by Yahid "Serial Killer" Rodriguez of Mexico while surfing the Internet, and thought to himself that those designs were incredible.

The collaboration between mimoco and Yahid Rodriguez on the Cosmos Series was

a novelty to the art scene. The truth that Yahid was just starting out at the time became a factor that contributed to mimico's popularity, making both an instant hit in design-conscious markets.

Mimobots are preloaded with character-related media content such as animation, games and music, all designed by talented people. Artists with which mimoco has teamed up include TADO, Jon Burgerman, Shawnimals, Dino Alberto, Mori Chack, Hanazuki, Happy Tree Friends, Sket One, Kim Koch, Devil Robots, Lili Chin and Brian McCarty, DJ DB, Biggies Broadband Studios, Peskimo and Penfold Plum.

Since then, Evan has also produced the Star Wars mimobot Series after a successful licensing deal with Lucas Films. The mimobots' Artists Series meanwhile, is an ongoing collaboration with influential artists and designers to produce special limited editions.

mimoco has begun another collaboration with Yahid Rodriguez on the first Pure Vinyl Art Toy – the core vimobot Series, presented in blind assortment (you won't know which toy you get till you open the box), based on Yahid's original Core mimobot Series.

artist / Evan Blaustein

location / Brookline • MA

website / www.mimoco.com

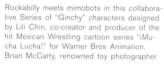

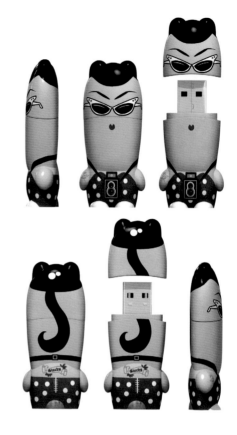

Rockabilly meets mimobots in this collaborative Series of "Ginchy" characters designed
by Lili Chin, co-creator and producer of the
hit Mexican Wrestling cartoon series "¡Mu-
cha Lucha!" for Warner Bros Animation.
Brian McCarty, renowned toy photographer

and director/producer provides an extra-
special cargo load for the series with his
quirky photo albums of the Ginchy friends'
Los Angeles adventures, set to a soundtrack
by Phofo.

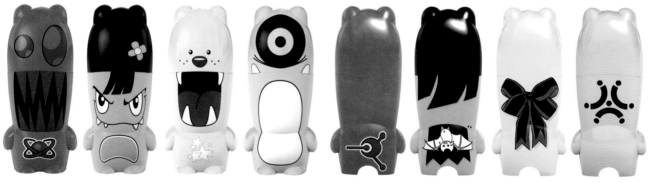

Core mimobots (Cosmos and goSeries)
design by / Yahid Rodriguez

01
02

01 / Ginchy Series Design
02 / Core mimobots
(Cosmos and goSeries) Design

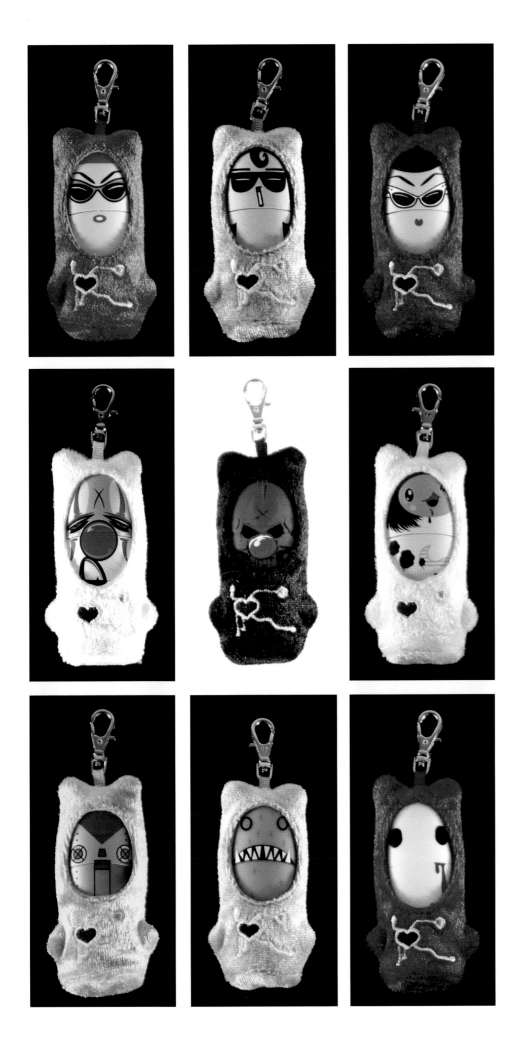

artist / NDEUR / Mathieu MISSIAEN • Charnel baz'art collective member

location / Paris • Toronto

website / www.ndeur.com / www.myspace.com/ndeur

GRAPHIC CONCEPT

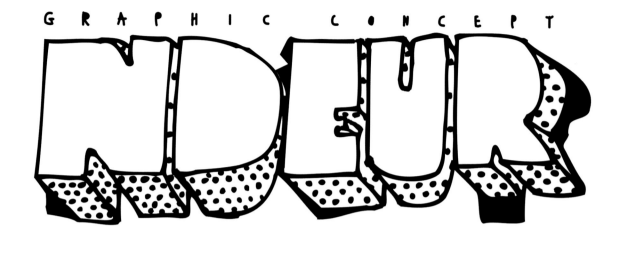

00 / Ladies Shoes Design

ORIGINAL CUTS:

NDEUR

www.ndeur.com

" I love to change material because I start to get bored very quickly with something. I love the adaptation of mediums and get totally into it. "

– Mathieu Missiaen, NDEUR –

Parisian artist Mathieu Missiaen is the painter for NDEUR, a shoe label he created during his stay in Toronto. He owns over 100 pairs of women's shoes of all heights and sizes in his small apartment, all made pretty with his paintings.

For Mathieu, vintage leather shoes aren't quite a fetish but actually works very well as a canvas instead. They are decorated using oil-based paints and varnished for protection against crude weathers. Imagine this precious mixture of paints, colours and shoes that contributes to Mathieu's one-of-a-kind style and popularity.

It's without a doubt that NDEUR doesn't belong to any look or scene. Instead, you can almost see ripples of different styles, from pop to graffiti-inspired motifs, formed by using the same basic treatment on the Mod-ish shoes.

"If you see my paintings, I don't have homogenous works," he says. "I love to change all the time but I don't try to look for a specific style that's only me who has it. If I could, I'd like to try to have it all."

Reaching out is easy for this member of the Charnel Baz'art collective. He has even created a huge following for his shoes with a MySpace account.

He is currently the 'it' designer in Toronto with a fast-growing fan base who love his flashy-and-fun approach to killer heels. He paint shoes as well as sneakers for sale at stores in Toronto (The Rage), Belgium (Etsy Online Store, Elle Flip), Los Angeles (Sneaker Pimps) and the Vans Shoe Show at OMY Gallery also in Toronto.

artist / NDEUR / Mathieu MISSIAEN • Chanel baz'art collective member

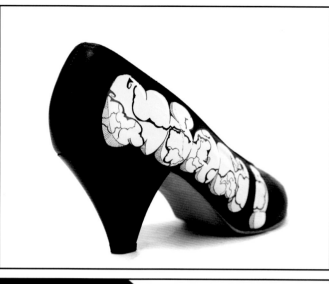
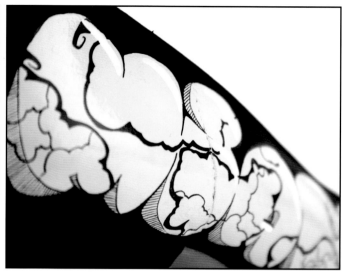

location / Paris • Toronto

website / www.ndeur.com / www.myspace.com/ndeur

00 / Ladies Shoes Design

artist / NDEUR / Mathieu MISSIAEN • Charnel baz'art collective member

location / Paris • Toronto

website / www.ndeur.com / www.myspace.com/ndeur

artist / NDEUR / Mathieu MISSIAEN • Charnel baz'art collective member

location / Paris • Toronto

website / www.ndeur.com / www.myspace.com/ndeur

PLATFORM2

12.05 - 13.01.06   'Chica' curator
16.01.06 - 03.02.06   Marc Freeman
06.02.06 - 24.02.06   Nadia Toukhsati
06.03.06 - 17.03.06   Ilana Payes
27.03.06 - 07.04.06   NEXT WAVE FESTIVAL
Mascot Project 'curator Estelle Ihasz

'2morrow's Kingdom Cargo' as part of
Container Village, Shed 14, Docklands
Presented by Pandarosa, Kongzilla & AKA ltd

10.04.06 - 28.04.06   Aimee Fairman
01.05 06 - 19.05.06   'Shelf Life' PAG Curated
22.05.06 - 09.06.06   Jessica New
12.06.06 - 30.06.06   Belle Bassin and Alasdair McLuckie
03.07.06 - 21.07.06   Scot Cotterell
24.07.06 - 11.08.06   Bethany Edwards
14.08.06 - 01.09.06   Ash Keating

Platform2
Campbell Arcade, Melbourne
(enter via Flinders St or Degraves St)

Mon - Fri 7am - 7pm
Sat 9am - 5pm

PLATFORM ARTISTS GROUP INC/STICKY
Shop 10 Campbell Arcade, Melbourne, 3000
(enter via Flinders St or Degraves St)
Wed - Fri 12 - 5pm
PO Box 310, Flinders Lane
Post Office Melbourne 8009
P/F: +61 3 9654 8559
E: platform@platform.org.au
www.platform.org.au

city of
Melbourne   Living
the Arts

ARTS
VICTORIA

Victoria
The Place To Be

DOUBLE ACE:
PANDAROSA
www.pandarosa.net

"

I believe the reason we have embraced vinyl so much is because it's never really been explored as an artistic medium. Vinyl has been limited in its use, usually related to BIG RED '50% OFF SALE' shop-front signage.

"

– Pandarosa Art and Design –

Hungarian Andrea Benyi and Ariel Aguilera from Chili migrated to Australia for a university stint and formed Pandarosa Art and Design shortly after their graduation in 2001. The studio specialises in creating graphics for a diverse range of artistic and music industry clients – and now welcomes vinyl as an artistic medium.

Even given their relatively recent formation, Pandarosa have been pretty busy since then. Their projects have included installations, projections, short films, website animation as well as interior decoration, for clients such as Adidas, Brochner Hotels, Die Gestalten Verlag, Eurolace, Eventlabs, Fat4, James Richardson Duty Free, Lee, Puma, 2 Arkitekter and Volkswagen. Together with others in a select group of international artists and designers, they were also commissioned to produce artworks for Copenhagen's Hotel Fox.

Many of their illustrations have appeared

on the pages of various Australian magazines including Black & White, Desktop and Yen as well as international titles like Neomu, Grafik, Icon and Frame to name a few. Besides a string of animation works shown in international film festivals, other graphic-based works have been highlighted in several publications such as Wonderland, Hidden Track (Die Gestalten Verlag), Graphics Alive (Victionary) and Dotmov 2004 (IDN).

Recently, they held an exhibition of vinyl works on wallpaper, using the medium to create canvas-like pieces instead of the usual interior/exterior mural-based works they'd been doing all this while. They've in fact started using adhesive vinyl extensively on interiors, exteriors, floors, glass and many other surfaces as well.

All in all, their style is mostly about creating an emotion or feeling rather than recognisable images. They are more about stimulating imagination than describing.

Ariel adds that by exploring a particular theme or finding the most lateral approach to a design, they also attempt to bring an element of chance and randomness into it, if ever that's possible.

Besides, they enjoy letting happy accidents take place because these keep things interesting and original. If, however, the vibe isn't right at the studio, a change in atmosphere always helps in giving them a burst of inspiration.

"We'd walk down the Yarra River and watch the rowers do their thing, or walk to the botanical gardens with a camera in hand. Otherwise, it's definitely music," says Ariel, the more experienced of the duo. She lists the beautiful lyrics of Nina Simone or Manu Chao as well as the atmospheric instrumental pieces by the Cinematic Orchestra or Fourtet as her favourites.

artist / Pandarosa • Ariel Aguilera / Andrea Benyi

location / Melbourne • Australia

website / www.pandarosa.net

artist / Pimpmyscoota

website / www.pimpmyscoota.com

00 / Scoota Skin Design

MOBILE GLOBETROTTER:
PIMPMYSCOOTA

www.pimpmyscoota.com

> " The Pimpmyscoota design community includes artists Kanardo, Luke Feldman, Front Panel Stripes, Koa, Nick Deakin, Angel D'Akimo, Chris Buzelli, Klutch, Stinger, Dolceq, Darren Goldman, Pierre Girard, Dolla, Bev Hogue, Wes Van Eeden and Jason Limon. "

– Pimpmyscoota –

What do Kanardo, Luke Feldman, Koa and Nick Deakin have in common? That's right, they've all created cool decals for pimpmyscoota! Decals, short for Decal-comania, are pattern transfers that can be used to decorate anything from hot rod automobiles to plastic models. In the case of pimpmyscoota, the pimping's got to be, what else, but classic retro Vespa PX scooters.

Pimpmyscoota founder and Vespa owner Dane Flighty generated this idea from his desire to create something extra cool and beguiling for his own bike. From the huge circle of talented artists and designers from different corners of the globe, Flighty began his search for the best to design the first series of PX decals. Today, designs from more than 17 artists are available on high quality long life outdoor grade vinyl that can withstand coarse weathers for at least 5 years.

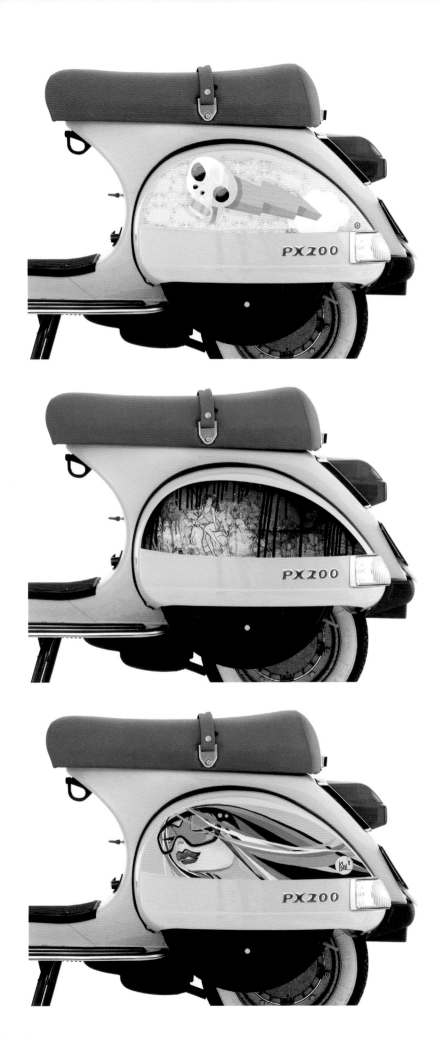

00 / Toys Design

ULTRA POP FASHION:
POTI POTI
www.potipoti.com

Silvia Salvador and Nando Cornejo are among Spain's best exports in graphics-focused fashion. Together, they are called Potipoti, which is all about illusory works, taking references from sources like musical duo Vainica Doble, classic cartoons from the past and fashion off the streets.

These two young Spanish designers and illustrators received their education in fine art in Salamanca. In 2001, they moved to Berlin, after which they formed a fashion company called Potipoti and started setting up gallery exhibitions and fashion shows.

Their designs are geometric, colourful and very much pop-based. Potipoti's clothing line is made in much the same way a birthday cake is, with love and colours, aimed at providing happiness to everyone who has them. The simple trace creatures on the clothing create kinky images of naivety, as well as mixed feelings of rage and tenderness.

There is always a personal style to each of Potipoti's collections. In its Spring/Summer 07 Inside Out Collection, the T-shirts, capes, skirts, dresses and polos were based on handmade illustrations, using ambiguity and almost childish illustrations as coloured prints on pieces of black and white fabrics.

Silvia and Nando like mixing their disciplines without inhibitions especially fashion, art and graphic design. So even if they regularly participate in cool fashion events such as the Bread & Butter trade show in Barcelona, they've also exhibited their illustrations in New York and Berlin, as well as DJed for Heineken's 2007 Festival Internacional de Benicassim (FIB). To put it succinctly, they liken their tastes to those of Henrik Vibskov, Andrea Crews and the multidisciplinary art group, Chicks on Speed.

The twenty-four-hour-a-day routine in Berlin inspires them. They chat on small details such as buying the best tomatoes in the Turkish market in Kreuzberg, getting on a boat ride in Plötzensee Lake, running into nice people on the street, or being at a good concert in a small illegal club. "Because the simplest things inspire us, or when lacking inspiration, we get ourselves a delicious avocado shake!"

artist / Potipoti * Silvia Salvador / Nando Cornejo

location / Berlin

website / www.potipoti.com

/ Skirts Design

Potipoti has won the contest Linea De from General Optica in Spain and our collection of glasses will be available in all General Optica's shops of Spain at the end of 2007

design by / Silvia Salvador y Nando Cornejo, potipoti
3D modeling by / Thomas-Eric Béliveau

00 / Glasses Design

Potipoti has won the contest Linea De from General Optica
in Spain and our collection of glasses will be available in all
General Optica's shops of Spain at the end of 2007

design by / Silvia Salvador y Nando Cornejo, potipoti
3D modeling by / Thomas-Eric Béliveau

LIVING CRAFT:
RYAN FRANK
www.ryanfrank.net

> 66
>
> I've started building a library of samples of interesting materials, particularly hemp and bamboo. I haven't found the uses for all of them at the moment, but hopefully one day the right project will allow me to do so.
>
> 99
>
> – Ryan Frank –

Product designer Ryan Frank prefers to just get on with his own stuff, whatever that may be, instead of doing what is already out there and tapping into current consumption patterns. He'd grown up and studied product design in Cape Town, completed his course in Zwolle, Holland, and then channeled his knowledge and a deep sense of belonging to culture, into his work in East London where he currently resides.

Ryan's creative, almost eccentric, flair for design was previously honed from working for a short period at Den Hartog Musch, a Dutch product company, as well as at leading architecture firm Alsop Architects. His furniture creations are conventional yet very personal and functionally sustainable.

"Perhaps, it's the bringing of a little bit of Africa with me to Europe that allowed my South African roots to trickle into many of my products," he reckons. "Or maybe it's the use of reclaimed, salvaged materials that are rusted, chipped, scratched and weathered for which my products are famous, but then again every designer is different."

One of his bestsellers happens to be the larger-than-life Hackney Shelf – an idea coming from a low-tech environment that is visually rich and refreshing. The shelving unit is to be exposed in the London streets, graffiti-ed upon then removed and built into a shelf when it matures.

"Where you get inspiration is important because it guides and nurtures the product's development. Inspiration is from random occurrences. I can get pangs of inspiration at any time of day and night," says Ryan.

"People like Dr. Seuss, Jamie Hewlett and Gary Larsen – they are all illustrators but have inspired me in the past, which I find interesting because I don't illustrate."

Things do get a little fuzzy sometimes in distinguishing where exactly his stand is in the design line. In spite of the difficulties or criticisms that were shoved into his face for his bold approach in product design, he is very much a determined person. To him, life's been a mix of excitement and lots of hard work to get to the top of the game.

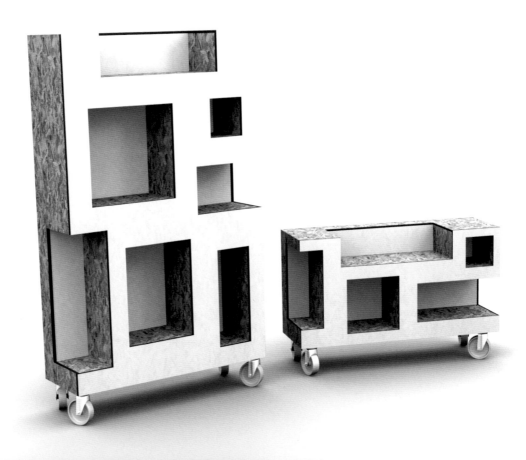

PICTURE BOOKS:
RYOJI ARAI
www.kingofmountain.info

> " In over 50 of his published children's books, it's without a doubt Ryoji Arai's works seem to flow freely from page to page. "

Ryoji Arai is described as one of Japan's leading contemporary illustrators with a big, almost childlike personality. He draws influences from folk tales and fables and dresses up many of his successful picture books with his own writings.

The discerning man in his 50s has contributed to a renewed interest in picture book reading with a style that is all his own: bold, magical and impulsive. In over 50 of his published children's books, it's without a doubt that his works seem to flow freely from page to page. The increasing demand for picture books from adults alike has been testament to the good humour and warmth spread throughout his pages.

Further recognition has come in the form of the Bologna Ragazzi Award at the Bologna Children's Book Fair in 1999 for "Dr. Do-Riddle in the Riddle Land". But it was in 2005 that he was named co-winner of the Astrid Lindgen memorial award, the world's most prestigious book prize for children's and young people's literature, named after the Swedish author of the Pippi Longstocking books.

Arai's latest picture book – "Refrain Refrain" – was published in 2005. It is pure novelty and depicts a main character who seeks adventures and all its craziness. In fact, this figure and his fellow characters have been given a new lease of life on mugs and plates, which are sold at King of Mountain's online shop.

Besides his own books, Arai has illustrated for The Angel Foundation which published A Forest Picture Book, with words composed by Japanese lyricist Hiroshi Osada.

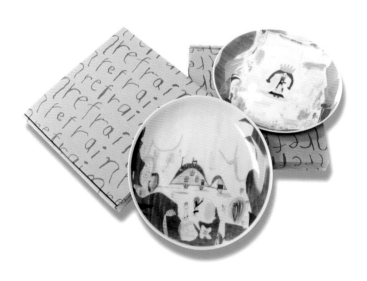

01

02 03

01 / Doodles Design
02 / Cups Design
03 / Dishes Design

00 / 3D Sculptures Display

MIKRO IN ITS ELEMENT:
SAMBUXTON
www.sambuxton.com

❝ The Mikro-House was originally an experiment, to construct a complete living unit from a single sheet...with some of my own work in it and a few extras like strings of hair in the bathroom and hand-cuffs hanging from the bed. ❞

– Sam Buxton –

Mikro-Man is Sam Buxton's design interpretation of science built from a chemical milling process he had discovered in the electronics industry. A flat fine stainless steel card unfolded into 3D sculptures, it was exhibited at London's Design Museum in 2001. Worldwide Co. liked the idea and collaborated with Buxton to mass produce the first in a series of Mikro fold-up sculptures.

This London native has since in his graduating years from the Royal College of Art mused much over science, design, art and astronomy. Before that, he'd studied furniture design at Middlesex University citing Tatsuo Miyajima and Louise Bourgeois as the inspiration to his own wonderful creations for the sculptural "Mikro-World".

The birth of Mikro-Man was actually intended to be a business card in Buxton's attempt to make a decent living in the business world. Instead, it was his biggest career break. From then on, he was dealing with people from Habitat, Swarovski Crystal, Vauxhall Motors, Kenzo Paris, Deutsche Bank, Range Rover, Bloomberg, Siemens and Reebok.

Buxton's licensed series of Mikro-Man were sell-outs. In 2003 he was commissioned by Design Museum Tank to engineer an installation of Mikro-City, a 24-hour glass box public exhibition space outside the museum. The boundaries between display screens and the physical environment fell apart with Buxton's art. A year later, he was nominated for Designer of the Year 2004 in the UK.

His biggest preoccupation is not in Mikro-Man or Mikro-City but the creation of Mikro-House, a miniature living unit complete with spaces and intricately detailed features of a kitchen, bathroom and living room. The Mikro miniatures are also based on the "snapshots of real life that people come to recognise". The challenge was to make it seamless and life-like.

The symbol of time passing also seems to intrigue him. The result of that was the usage of electroluminescent technology in a series of object experiments he called Surface Intelligent Objects (SIOS) which attempts to combine information display onto the surfaces of objects, thus creating active surfaces on familiar objects around us.

00 / 3D Sculptures Display

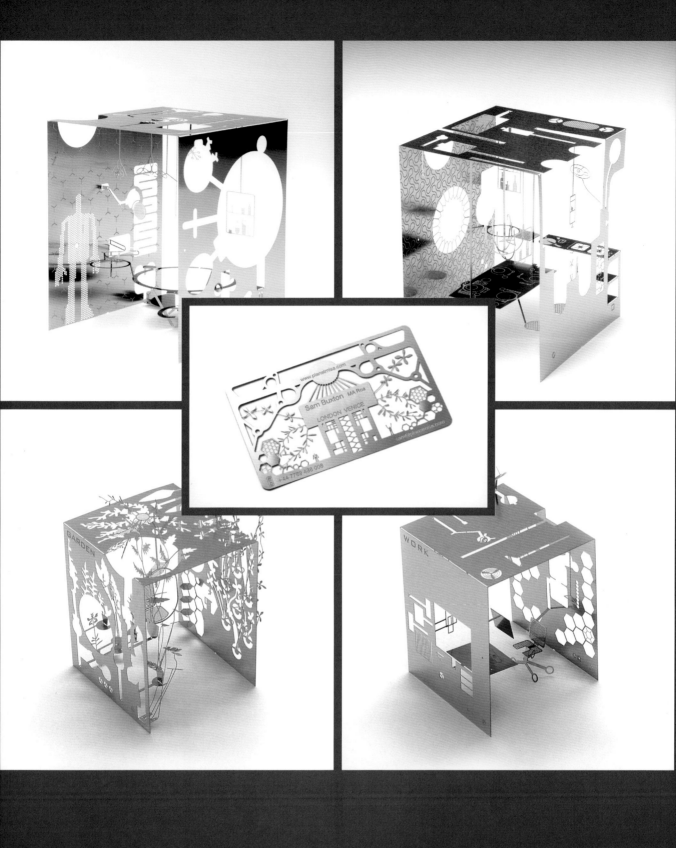

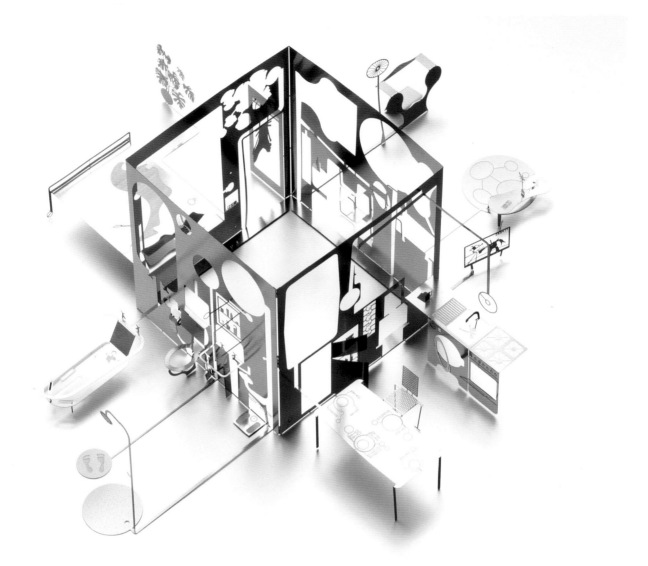

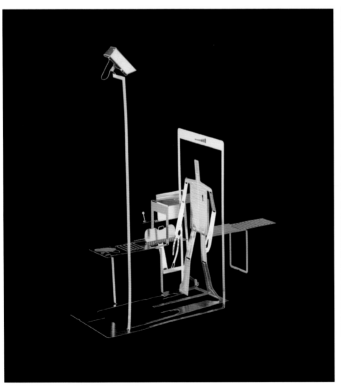

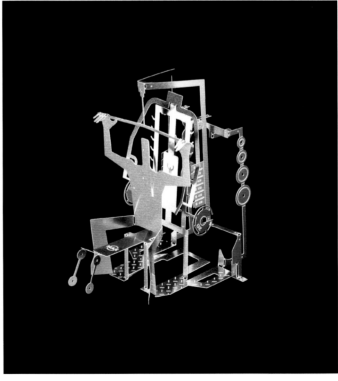

00 / 3D Sculptures Design

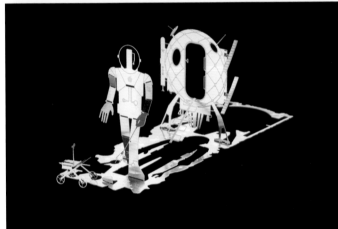

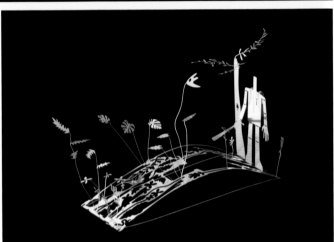

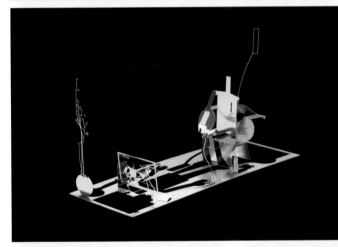

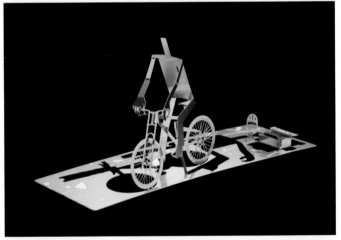

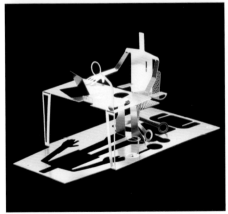

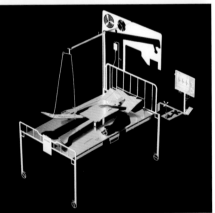

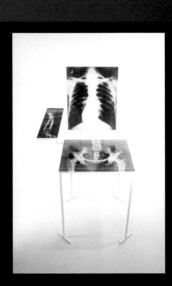
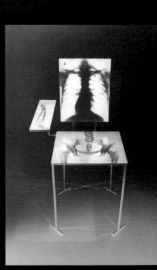

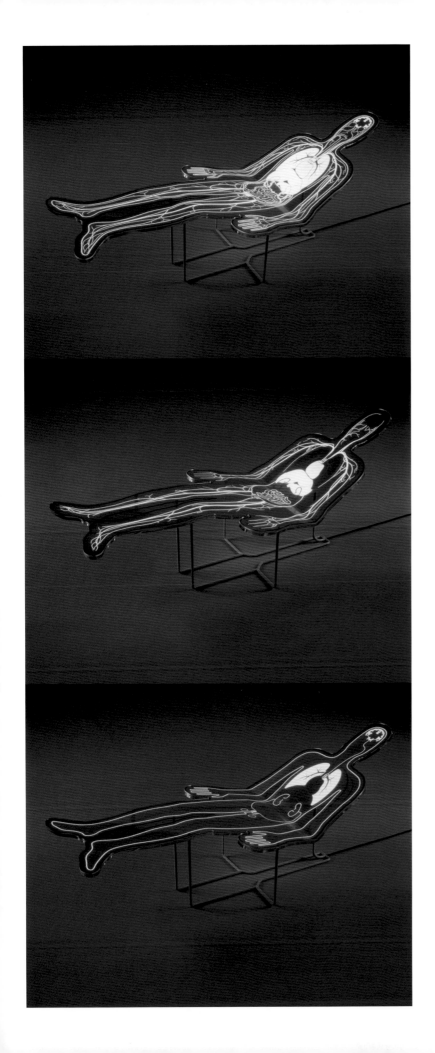

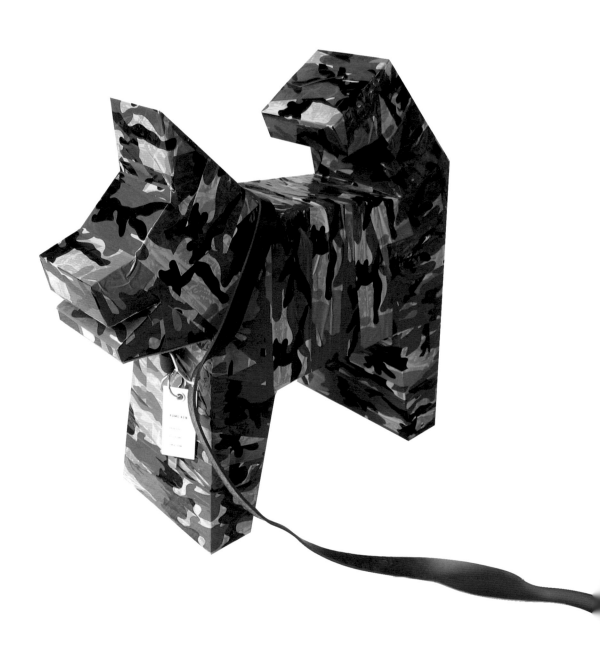

> " I love wood and the limitless possibilities of weaving, but also the uniformity of synthetic materials and techniques that are not labour-intensive. "
>
> – Sonia Chow –

Uni, named after the Japanese word for sea urchin, was created by Canadian born Sonia Chow who lives in Tokyo. The product's ability to lighten up a dull space is worth its mention in I.D. Magazine, not least for its basic use of a long garden hose and cable ties woven together.

"Growing up, I thought I should choose a career that was practical. When I was in high school, I focused on maths and sciences. Then, I started university as a chemical engineering major but soon found out that it wasn't for me," she says. After that, she decided to follow her instincts and focus on design.

Now, she is a successful designer, having already notched up 19 awards for graphic and furniture design, and is constantly moving from Tokyo to other parts of Japan and Hong Kong. Every time she experiences this kind of upheaval, she reflects on what has happened in her life. She is amazed at how some designers can pinpoint the exact moment they began pursuing their professions, but scratches her head when she tries to recall a specific moment which she could call an enlightenment.

"It feels more gradual, like an adventure which continues to unravel non-stop," expresses Sonia.

In fact, when she realised that doing her own thing was more "practical" and fun, she switched from an office environment to her own establishment, Sonia Chow Studio.

As seen at her recent shows at several design and art events in Canada and Japan, Sonia continues to design more functional furniture sets and fashion accessories made from varied textiles and materials. Be it traditional designs or objects for the mass market, the process is appealing to her, considering that her Western origins, her own quirks as well as her interest in the Asian way of life, are all beginning to merge into one.

Two Bits for example was produced for CTE05, an alternative art exhibition in Tokyo. It featured two stamps which create lively letterforms in their negative space, spelling out equally playful musings on Japanese pop culture. Kamo Ken the designer dog meanwhile, was a collaboration between Sonia and D. Akihabara Temporary Museum, Tokyo.

"I think the important thing is to be true to yourself and do the things you love. It's not a great idea to worry too much about trends or to focus heavily on what seems to be the popular thing. It would just invite frustration."

artist / Sonia Chow

location / Tokyo • Hong Kong

website / www.soniachowstudio.com

01

02

01 / Kamo Ken Design
02 / Kamo Ken's Album Design

Two Bits

This piece was produced for CET05, an alternative art exhibition in Tokyo. The text was written to suit the lively spirit of the letterforms, and contains playfully worded musings about Japanese pop culture. After printing, the panels were rearranged to redirect the attention from the content to the essence of the form, though it's possible to figure out the original layout of the panels using colour and spacing as clues.

00 / Bag Poster Design

JAPANESE TO THE CORE:
TOKIDOKI
www.tokidoki.it

" The part of my job I will always prefer doing is the hand sketch and painting. I like most of my designs and it's just wonderful to study the ways that can make my art work, whether it be on a piece of clothing, a timepiece, a shoe or a booth at a trade fair. "

– Simone Legno, creator of Tokidoki –

From the day Simone Legno's Tokidoki characters were spotted by the co-founder of Hard Candy Cosmetics in early 2003 to the moment he accepted the company's offer for a career move from Rome to Los Angeles, this was the journey that established Tokidoki as an international lifestyle brand.

When the opportunity came it was very much unexpected however, as Tokidoki had only started out as a personal website. Yet, Hard Candy Cosmetics were optimistic to conceptualise Tokidoki as a brand. There's been no looking back since and Simone has animated his Tokidoki characters on apparel, art, vinyl toys, skateboards, iSkins, watches, knitwear, denims, sportswear, bags and accessories.

Successfully branded to cater to the demanding worldwide market for lifestyle and "in style" products, Tokidoki is so well-known that LeSportSac jumped in for a long-term contract with the graphic designer. After all, Tokidoki has become cult iconography for the young and edgy, symbolising the aspect of Japanese culture, that is, bright colours and eclectic characters.

His other clients included MTV, John Galliano, Toyota, Renault, Daihatsu, BenQ, Microsoft, Narcotic Bureau Singapore and many more. Volkswagen even selected the rooms he designed at the Hotel Fox as a "hot spot" meeting room for the press.

Along the way, Simone has also conquered half of the world with several appearances in the media, especially Vogue, Elle, Marie Claire, WWD, Vanity Fair, XFuns, Computer Arts and books by Taschen and Die Gestalten Verlag.

Simone says, "My design is my diary. I live for what I do and sometimes I don't consider it as a job but rather a life-fulfilling thing. Tokidoki is the only way I can communicate a positive feeling to as many people out there as possible."

Perhaps, a little history of his discovery of Tokidoki could help explain what he means by "a positive feeling". Tokidoki means "sometimes" in Japanese. It is so named because it's believed that moments can change one's destiny either by chance or by a new encounter.

Tokidoki is a human interpretation of Simone's frame of reference in life – experiences, good friends, his classical art painter mother, joy, misery – and injected with innate talent, overflowing passion, and a dreamy personality.

00 / Series Bags Design

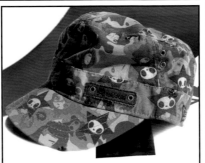

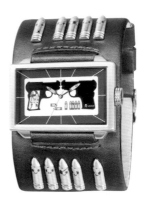

01 / Caps Design
02 / Watches Design

00 / Pool Booth Display

00 / Keinu Swing Design

DESIGN FOR LIFE:
TUNTO DESIGN
www.tunto.fi

66 Wood is my main material and I am good working at it. I also appreciate it as an element of the earth; it is warm and is a living material, sort of like a mother. Other materials I prefer are metal and glass. Glass is the most beautiful material you can find, melted glass especially, for its shining glow is very beautiful. 99

– Mikko Kärkkäinen, Tunto Design –

Finland and its history in design has, since the 50's and 60's, been fabulous and inspirational to the generations who have followed. Pioneering works like the furniture of Alvar Aalto, the dishes of Littala and clothes by Marimekko have formed part of the Finnish everyday environment and paved the way for today's players like Mikko Kärkkäinen of Tunto Design.

Nevertheless, they have also created a pretty competitive environment in design. "The fact is, it is extremely difficult to make a breakthrough with many other talented designers in the market, but the towering number of them is a positive sign for us too because we are then forced to do our best and stand out by working on better products and having strong faith in what we do," expounds Mikko.

Educated at Lahti Institute of Design, Finland, Mikko also credits his achievements to his father, late mother and sister for providing him with a happy childhood.

Yet, one probably can't fault his own canny timing and perhaps an element of destiny as well. After having worked at a carpentry workshop for eight years, opportunity at one point knocked and Mikko bought over the workshop. He wanted something for a change but couldn't figure what that would be. Yet, he mustered up the courage and pursued his desire to make Tunto Design a reality.

Working with different suppliers and freelance designers, the results have been new products that have never been made before, the likes of the M3 seat, Hoover lamp as well as the Skede chair, which cleverly employs what looks like a skateboard as its back rest.

And they've not come away without attracting their fair share of admirers. So far, Tunto products have been exhibited at New York Design Week, Tokyo Furniture Fair and Stockholm Furniture Fair in 2007; as well as Children's Play – Nordic Design Exhibition in Korea and Helsinki Design Week both in 2006.

Other than design, Mikko has a family, wife and a lovely baby girl to continue to make a difference to his life. Most of the time however, he regards himself as an individual operator and feels lucky to have been the sole navigator of his path. Says Mikko, "When I look back, I feel I have managed to make good desicions based on my intuitions."

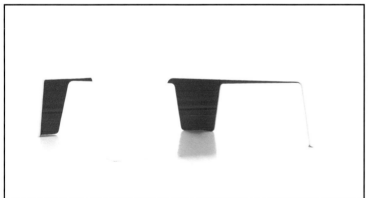

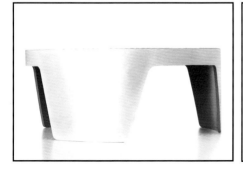

01

02 03

04

01 / Skede Design
02 / Vuokko Pink Table Design
03 / Hoover Design
04 / Kukka Table Design

"SUPER-BASTARD" TOY MAKER:

UNDOBOY

www.undoboy.com

> " I grew up in Malaysia with a Chinese background. For me, Chinese characters are a form of art, and the composition of symbols is truly amazing, which influences me. Also, a good conversation can really inspire me for a change in perspective. "
>
> – Undoboy –

Originally from Malaysia, Undoboy is now in Portland, Oregon where he works as art director in ad agency Wieden+Kennedy. Previously, he was art director at J Walter Thomson, New York, and before that, had a short stint as designer at Miami's Crispin Porter + Bogusky in 2005. All these in the span of three years.

In September 2006, his debut Super-Bastard Box Art Characters designer toys earned him a merit from the New York-based Art Directors' Club (ADC) in the Graphic Design Corporate and Promotional Design category.

Designed to promote and build a brand identity for himself at the time, this series of 16 toys are made out of heavy card stocks with matt lamination, and feature a total of 64 characters. They had originated from Undoboy's interest in iconography and character design, and feature gradients of colours as the most used and explored design element. The result is "boxy super fun".

The graduate with a Bachelor of Fine Arts (BFA) in Graphic Design from the Ringling School of Art and Design had grown up in the realm of Japanese manga and Hong Kong pop culture. The Superflat movement, postmodernism, and the intertwining of art and pop culture, have also had a very strong impact on Undoboy's beliefs.

Undoboy tries to retain that feeling of joy in the things he does and works around this to make the most out of creative freedom. Inspiration can also come from a brief walk outside the studio or watching a movie. Perhaps, he might create a new series of Super-Bastard Box Art Characters based on an entertaining blockbuster next.

For his Super-Bastard Toy concept as well as campaigns such as VW Features, BK Whopperettes, Mini Roofstudio, Mini Rally Race, BK Coqroq Integrated and GTI Features, Undoboy has garnered awards at prestigious competitions such as the Advertising Club of New York's Andy Award, the Clio Awards, the One Club's One Show Interactive awards, the Webby Awards (presented to the "world's best websites"), Cannes Cyber Lions (the awards for the online category at this advertising festival) and the London International Awards.

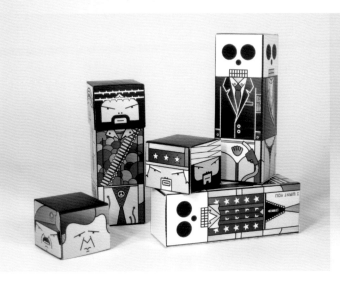

artist / Karl Emilio Pircher / Fidel Peugeot / Sylvia Sauermann

location / Vienna • Austria

website / www.walking-chair.com

designer / Karl Emilio Pircher / Fidel Peugeot / Sylvia Sauermann

00 / 'PET Light' Series Lighting Design

MASTER OF FONTS:
WALKING-CHAIR

www.walking-chair.com

"
Our constant and intensive grafting, mixing, merging and editing, is perhaps closer to the way music is combined to create new forms. When it does, an iconic concept can be tempered with, added to another and produce an entirely new idea: 1 + 1 = NEW.
"

– Walking-Chair Design Studio GmbH –

In the eyes of Karl Emilio Pircher and Fidel Peugeot, a good chair is good design like any other furniture. It has to be achieved through precision, knowledge and passion. In parallel, Austria's Walking-Chair Design Studio GmbH is meant to be a support structure for all kinds of products, and created with as much care. In fact, Fidel wants to introduce designs of various ambitious designers from all around the world alongside the studio's own.

Swiss born filmmaker Fidel met mechanical engineer turned product designer Karl Emilio six years ago while working as freelance designers for the Lomographic Society on a new type of handset. Back in 1995, "Designer of the Year" for Salon du Meuble de Paris was awarded to Karl Emilio, a holder of Masters of Mechanical Engineering and a degree in product design at the University of Applied Arts in Vienna.

Together with Fidel, he has after all created some great designs. Their designs such as the Monte Bello chair, Ping Meets Pong

round table and Tooltime utensils radiate pure irony. They have also designed font families, cultural exhibitions and shop interiors for BMW/mini, Lomographic Society, Colette Paris, E&Y Japan, GQ USA and Wallpaper UK magazines, Albertina Museum and other Italian, Swiss, German and increasingly local Austrian companies.

In a collaboration with the Aram Gallery for a first solo show in London last year, Walking-Chair launched five new products, a portfolio showcase of their projects and a series of fonts. The exhibition reflected the studio atmosphere through its unique site-specific installation. The ground was also an opportunity to launch the studio's online platform "walking things from Vienna".

Along with the appointment of Sylvia Sauermann as the head of Walking-Chair architecture department, the studio has now expanded to even take on a number of building projects including a leisure and water park in Bosnia-Herzegovina.

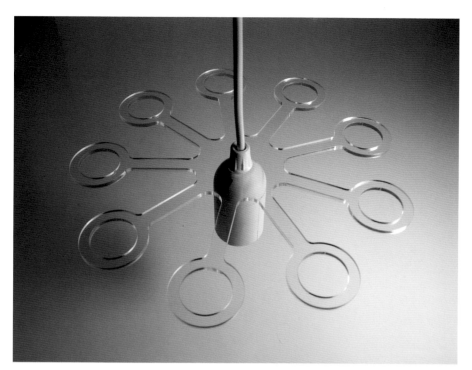

designer / Karl Emilio Pircher
/ Fidel Peugeot
/ Sylvia Sauermann

designer / Karl Emilio Pircher
/ Fidel Peugeot
/ Sylvia Sauermann

01
02

01 / 'PET Light' Series Lighting Design
02 / 'My First Chandelier' Series Lighting Design

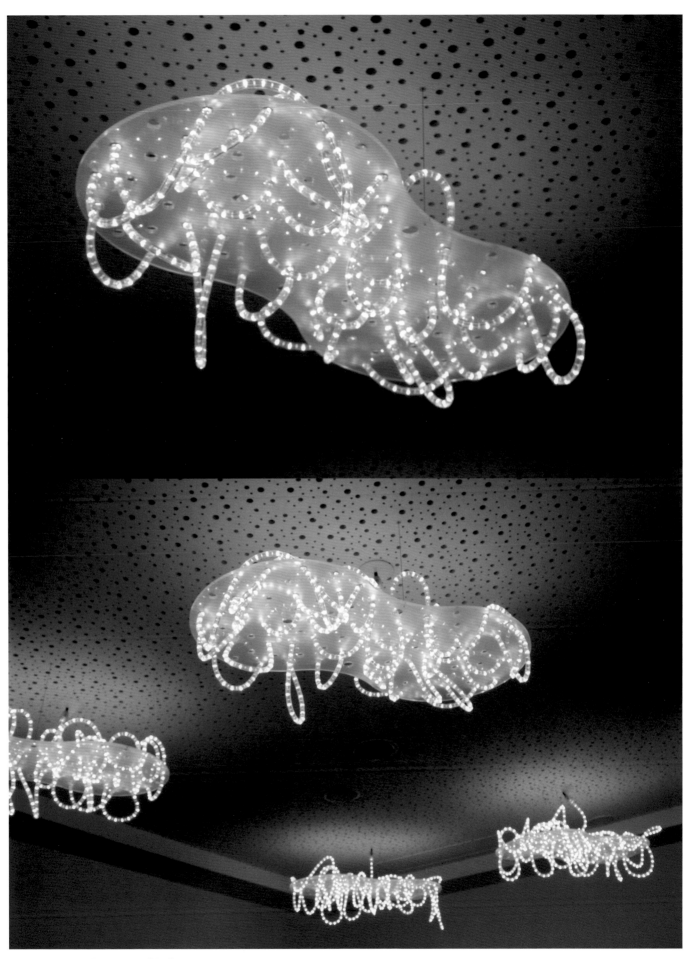

artist / Karl Emilio Pircher / Fidel Peugeot / Sylvia Sauermann

location / Vienna • Austria

website / www.walking-chair.com

designer / Karl Emilio Pircher / Fidel Peugeot
/ Sylvia Sauermann

designer / Karl Emilio Pircher
/ Fidel Peugeot
/ Sylvia Sauermann

designer / Karl Emilio Pircher
/ Fidel Peugeot
/ Sylvia Sauermann

01 / 'See You' Mirror Design
02 / 'Message People'
Series Note Clip Design

1_ collect your empty 0,5 L PET bottles
2_ clean the empty PET bottles
3_ shrink the PET bottles with heat and make a pin
4_ drill a hole in your wall
5_ fix the BOTTELBOY with a screw in the hole
6_ fill the shrunk PET bottle with nice things
7_ turn in the filled bottle in the BOTTLEBOY
8_ hang your things (hats, bags & clothes) on the pin
9_ relax, enjoy with BOTTLEBOY

MANIFESTO BOTTLEBOY

A NEW WARDROBE SYSTEM FOR HATS, BAGS & CLOTHES

designer / Karl Emilio Pircher
/ Fidel Peugeot
/ Sylvia Sauermann

artist / Karl Emilio Pircher / Fidel Peugeot / Sylvia Sauermann

location / Vienna • Austria

website / www.walking-chair.com

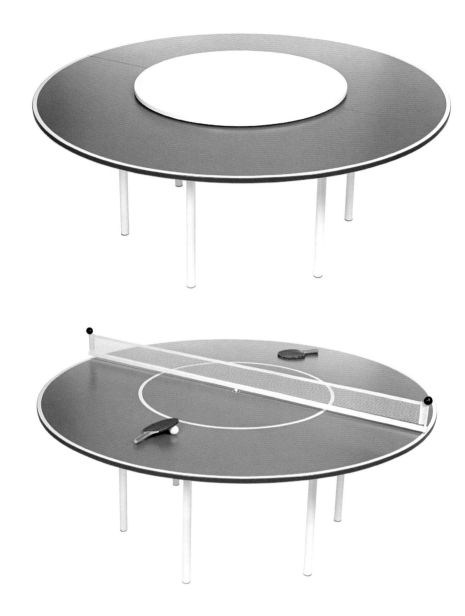

00 / 'Ping Meet Pong' Table Design

artist / Karl Emilio Pircher / Fidel Peugeot / Sylvia Sauermann

location / Vienna • Austria

website / www.walking-chair.com

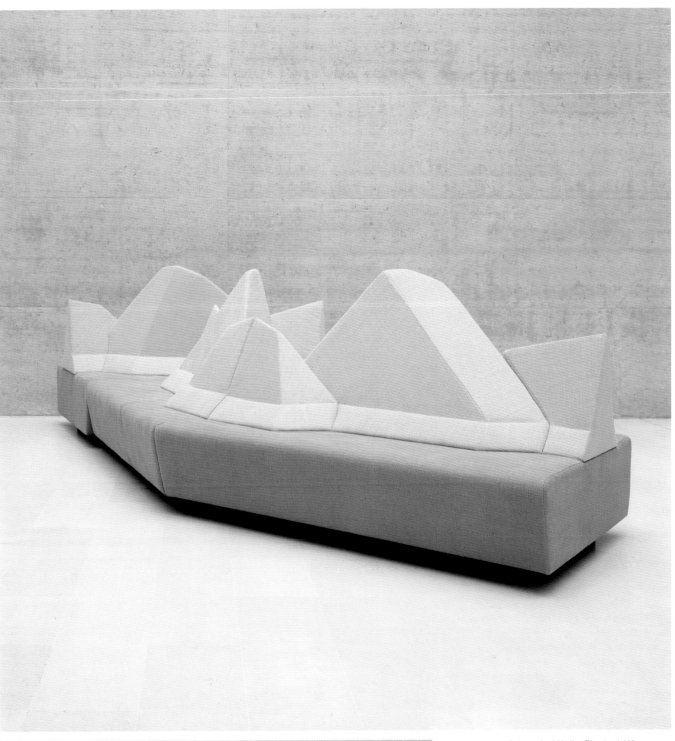

photography / Nadine Blanchard / Vienna
design by / Karl Emilio Pircher / Fidel Peugeot

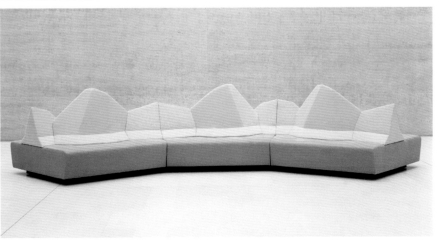

artist / Karl Emilio Pircher / Fidel Peugeot / Sylvia Sauermann

location / Vienna • Austria

website / www.walking-chair.com

designer / Karl Emilio Pircher
/ Fidel Peugeot
/ Sylvia Sauermann

00 / 'Banja Luka Chair' Design

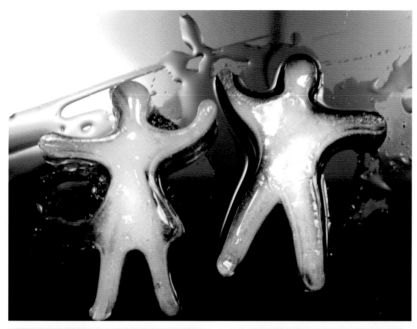

artist / Karl Emilio Pircher / Fidel Peugeot / Sylvia Sauermann

location / Vienna • Austria

website / www.walking-chair.com

designer / Karl Emilio Pircher
/ Fidel Peugeot

designer / Karl Emilio Pircher
/ Fidel Peugeot

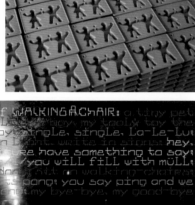

01 / 'My Bye-Bye'
Ice Shell Design

02 / 'Voice Of Walking-Chair'
CD Design

designer / Karl Emilio Pircher
/ Fidel Peugeot

00 / 'Pin Up' Design

single

single, single: La _ Le _ Lu
single, single: i Love you
single, single: c'est La vie
single, single: come with me
WALKINGЯCHAIR

designer / Karl Emilio Pircher / Fidel Peugeot

01

02

01 / '4T' Tea Table Design
02 / 'Single' Doll Design

00 / Wallpaper

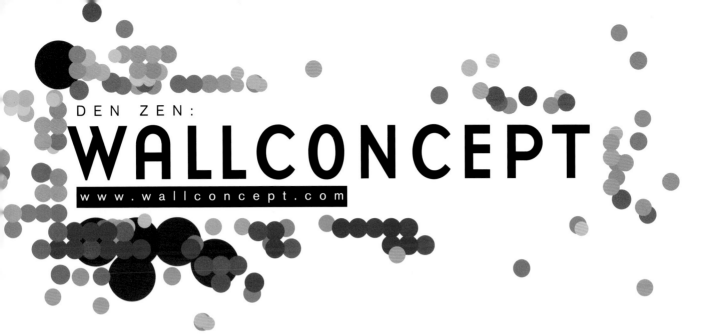

> " Wallconcept Lab is almost like a "den" – a collection of samples. At the moment we're working on patterns applied onto luxurious plexi/acrylic glass plates with chrome-finished distance spacers...as well as applied onto textiles. "

– Wallconcept –

If there is one thing to call revolutionary in design, that would be Swedish-based Wallconcept. Still relatively new on the market, founder Kostas Karatanasis and partner-cum-creative director Valentin Melstrom, made headlines with their easy-to-use applicable technique in wallpaper designing, championing mediums such as vinyl and stencil.

Perhaps you've seen many kinds of wallpaper designs before in your life, especially in Hollywood movies, TV programmes, salons or stage shows. If not, you've probably seen some created by Wallconcept in FRAME magazine, Elle Décor UK edition as well as other Swedish magazines.

The basis of Wallconcept appears striking in terms of their user-friendly identity and that the inspiring motifs intertwine between fashion and function, technology and practicality, revolutionary and ideal. Karatanasis is indeed taking wallpaper design seriously in his abode, to say the least. He reckons any inexperienced user can do a professional job with stencil – only when guided with a manual instruction book.

Certainly, people of today are very much interested in the colourful and do-it-yourself appeal of products. Take Wallconcept Vinyl for example. The vinyl foil used in this collection is available in a spectrum of sensational colours giving the illusion of a painted wall pattern.

Staying true to their company's tagline which reads "bring life to your walls", Karatanasis has worked alongside with Melstrom to create yet another unique, big-sized sticker stencil (Wallconcept Stencil), making wall painting less a chore (and almost zero smudges to the wall).

It was sheer coincidence that Karatanasis' friends liked what they saw as murals on his painted walls. Those motifs expressed what he had in mind about street art, fashion, magazines and movies of the moment. That masterpiece definitely landed him in the business of Wallconcept with Melstrom.

00 / Wallpaper Design

00 / Clothes Design

CHILD'S LOVE:
WE ARE AIKO

www.weareaiko.com

> " My story is a mix of luck, circumstances, facts and truths. I like materials that I cannot control. I like the randomness of certain elements. "
>
> – Niko Stumpo, creator of We Are Aiko –

Born to a Norwegian mother and an Italian father, much of Niko's work has an element of youthfulness to it. We Are Aiko is simply derived from the personal stories of the designer himself that were brought to life on canvas and textile.

Often described as an emotive and impulsive person, Niko has in his years spent time skating and sketching. After a two-year stint as an art director at W+K Amsterdam, he has now built his own business in web design, illustration and graphic design.

We Are Aiko is Niko Stumpo's brand created along with a good friend in 2001. Aiko was named to mean the child of love. Hanazuki, meanwhile, is another brainchild of the former pro skater which was featured in mimoco's "One Love" mimobot limited edition (Artists Series 2007).

At We Are Aiko, a symbiotic relationship between the brand and a group of col-

laborators is able to develop vigorously. Unlimited and free, We Are Aiko explores Niko's drawings, collaborations with other designers, and experiments with potential media whilst successfully creating a brand that's universal and collective.

Emotions have an impact on the ever changing design scene and he's just a part of the huge puzzle. "Part of the group, yes, but unique, like everyone else," as he describes it.

Niko's random works shown at We Are Aiko stir interest and positive feedback from the public and professionals alike. His character designs are distinctively adorable, designed with childlike graphics or drawn from make-believe. Behind all that creativity twirling and twisting inside his mind he can even make clay look smart, cool and all the rage.

artist / W+K Tokyolab • Woog • Eric Cruz / Klaus Haapaniemi / Sophie Toulouse / Grassstudio

website / www.bigbrosworkshop.com / www.utterubbish.com

corrugated
paper bin and folders

Packaging material made from layers of thick paper, the top layer of which is alternately grooved and ridged for added strength and rigidity.

段ボール製ごみ箱・フォルダ

梱包素材は厚紙を層にして作られています。
表層は交互に凹凸がつけられ強度と剛性が加えられています。

useless poster

Corrugated Paper Bin / design by W+K Tokyo Lab & Grassstudio
Corrugated Paper Folders / design by Eboy, W+K Tokyo Lab & Klaus Haapaniemi

> " It's really good to bring more attention to this idea, and try to change the outlook of 'Green thinking' into something more contemporary. "
>
> – Klaus Haapaneimi –

"useless = use less"

Where is design headed in the future? These questions are increasingly being asked by consumers and designers as the realities of living in a consumer society, where older goods are thrown out as soon as newer ones can be bought has taken a toll on the environment. Utterubbish is 'a witty review of recycling, redemption and recourse through design.'

To remedy and re-examine this impact, with the aim of creating a future that is sustainable and eco-logically friendly is the impetus for Territory's collaboration with Utterubbish Pte Ltd at this November's Singapore Design Festival. The concept behind the show, is to explore alternative methods of design, taking in account the use of a minimalist approach (Less is More), the catch phrase is "useless = use less" and recycled material in the creating and fashioning of the product.

artist / W+K TokyoLab • Woog • Eric Cruz / Klaus Haapaniemi / Sophie Toulouse / Grasstudio

website / www.bigbrosworkshop.com / www.utterrubbish.com

artist / W+K Tokyolab • Woog • Eric Cruz / Klaus Haapaneimi / Sophie Toulouse / Grasstudio

website / www.bigbrosworkshop.com / www.utterubbish.com

artist / W+K Tokyolab • Woog • Eric Cruz / Klaus Haapaneimi / Sophie Toulouse / Grasstudio

website / www.bigbrosworkshop.com / www.utterubbish.com

00 / Clothes Design

artist / W+K Tokyolab • Woog • Eric Cruz / Klaus Haapaneimi / Sophie Toulouse / Grasstudio

website / www.bigbrosworkshop.com / www.utterubbish.com

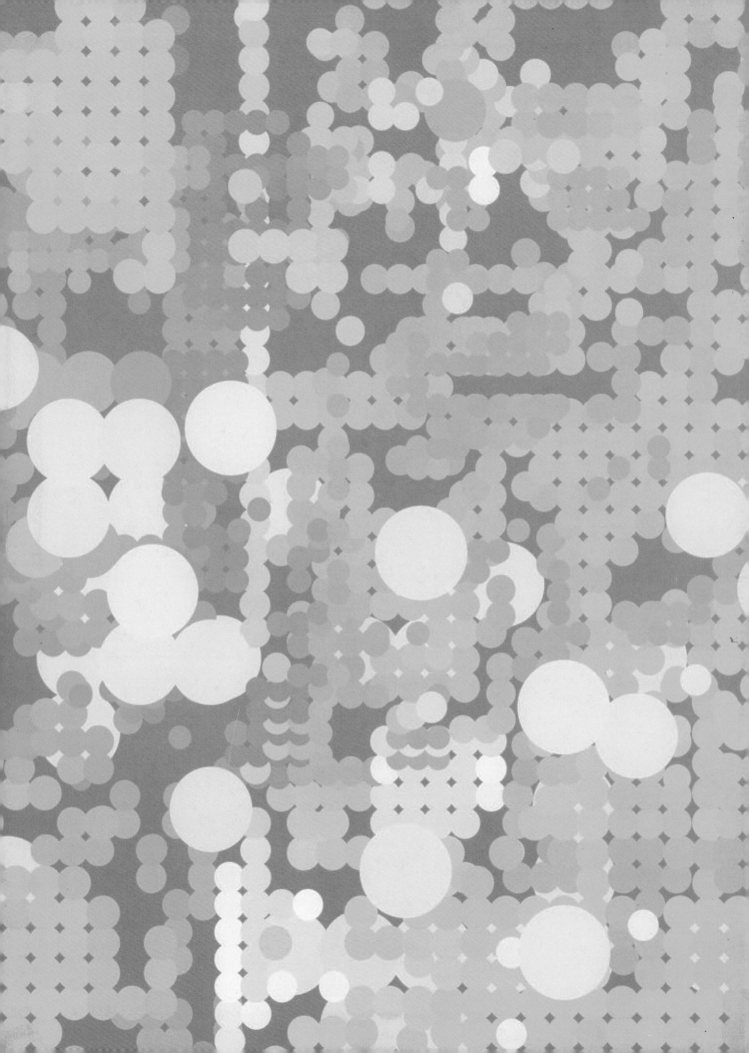